A Brain worth Million Dollars!

Worth knowing Ideas of Rich People who were not Born Rich!

It's your time to be… Rich!

By Sanyam Sadana

Preface

Are you born in a middle-class family? That's excellent! Or, are you born in a poor family? That's outstanding!

I'm not joking! I just want to tell you, and will be telling you throughout this book, that how interesting it is to born poor, and then, just by the power of your brain, which is still thinking how to be at the top of the world (am I wrong?), you will be seriously rich!

Yes, believe me or not, but most of today's billionaires were born poor. You can be one of them, can't you?

The book which you hold in your hands is a guide to ideas that made many rich! Thus, here are twenty six biographies and success-stories that will surely provoke the greedy you and pretty ideas will flash in your mind which will, if you are lucky enough, make you rich!

In the end, I have added the Becoming Rich Process, which is like a little step-by-step guide to get you at the top!

And one more thing, don't worry if you are not in a habit to read. The biographies are short and point-to-point (as I think!).

Table of Content:

Walt Disney

Walter Elias Disney was born in Chicago on December 5, 1901, the year in which the occupancy of the White House passed to 'that damned cowboy' the exuberant, ebullient Teddy Roosevelt.

Walt's optimism came from his unique ability to see the entire picture. His views and visions, came from the fond memory of yesteryear, and persistence for the future. Walt loved history. As a result of this, he didn't give technology to us piece by piece, he connected it to his ongoing mission of making life more enjoyable, and fun. Walt was our bridge from the past to the future.

During his 43-year Hollywood career, which spanned the development of the motion picture industry as a modern American art, Walter Elias Disney established himself and his innovations as a genuine part of Americana.

A pioneer and innovator, and the possessor of one of the most fertile and unique imaginations the world has ever known. Walt Disney could take the dreams of America, and make them come true. He was a creator, a imaginative, and aesthetic person. Even thirty years after his death, we still continue to grasp his ideas, and his creations, remembering him for everything he's done for us.

Later, after Walt's birth, the Disney family moved to Marceline, Missouri. Walt lived out most of his childhood here. Walt had a very early interest in drawing, and art. When he was seven years old, he sold small sketches, and drawings to nearby neighbors. Instead of doing his school work Walt doodled pictures of animals, and nature. His knack for creating enduring art forms took shape when he talked his sister, Ruth, into helping him paint the side of the family's house with tar. Walter Elias Disney was born on December 5, 1901 in Chicago Illinois, to his father, Elias Disney, an Irish-Canadian, and his mother, Flora Call Disney, who was of German-American descent. Walt was one of five children, four boys and a girl.

Close to the Disney family farm, there were Santa Fe Railroad tracks that crossed the countryside. Often Walt would put his ear against the tracks, to listen for approaching trains. Walt's uncle, Mike Martin, was a train engineer who worked the route between Fort Madison, Iowa, and Marceline. Walt later worked a summer job with the railroad, selling newspapers, popcorn, and sodas to travelers.

During his life Walt would often try to recapture the freedom he felt when aboard those trains, by building his own miniature train set. Then building a 1/8-scale backyard railroad, theCarolwood Pacific or Lilly Bell.

Besides his other interests, Walt attended McKinley High School in Chicago. There, Disney divided his attention between drawing and photography, and contributing to the school paper. At night he attended the Academy of Fine Arts, to better his drawing abilities.

Walt discovered his first movie house on Marceline's Main Street. There he saw a dramatic black-and-white recreation of the crucifixion and resurrection of Christ.

During these "carefree years" of country living young Walt began to love, and appreciate nature and wildlife, and family and community, which were a large part of agrarian living. Though his father could be quite stern, and often there was little money, Walt was encouraged by his mother, and older brother, Roy.

Even after the Disney family moved to Kansas City, Walt continued to develop and flourish in his talent for artistic drawing. Besides drawing, Walt had picked up a knack for acting and performing. At school he began to entertain his friends by imitating his silent screen hero, Charlie Chaplin. At his teachers invitation, Walt would tell his classmates stories, while illustrating on the chalk board. Later on, against his father's permission, Walt would sneak out of the house at night to perform comical skits at local theaters.

During the fall of 1918, Disney attempted to enlist for military service. Rejected because he was under age, only sixteen years old at the time. Instead, Walt joined the Red Cross and was sent overseas to France, where he spent a year driving an ambulance and chauffeuring Red Cross officials. His ambulance was covered from stem to stern, not with stock camouflage, but with Disney cartoons.

Once he returned from France, he wanted to pursue a career in commercial art, which soon lead to his experiments in animation. He began producing short animated films for local businesses, in Kansas City. By the time Walt had started to create The Alice Comedies, which was about a real girl and her adventures in an animated world, Walt ran out of money, and his company Laugh-O-Grams went bankrupted. Instead of giving up, Walt packed his suitcase and with his unfinished print of The Alice Comedies in hand, headed for Hollywood to start a new business. He was not yet twenty-two.

The early flop of The Alice Comedies inoculated Walt against fear of failure; he had risked it all three or four times in his life. Walt's brother, Roy O. Disney, was already in California, with an immense amount of sympathy and encouragement, and $250. Pooling their resources, they borrowed an additional $500, and set up shop in their uncle's garage. Soon, they received an order from New York for the first Alice in Cartoonland(The Alice Comedies) featurette, and the brothers expanded their production operation to the rear of a Hollywood real estate office. It was Walt's enthusiasm and faith in himself, and others, that took him straight to the top of Hollywood society.

Although, Walt wasn't the typical Hollywood mogul. Instead of socializing with the "who's who" of the Hollywood entertainment industry, he would stay home and have dinner with his wife, Lillian, and his daughters, Diane and Sharon. In fact, socializing was a bit boring to Walt Disney. Usually he would dominate a conversation, and hold listeners spellbound as he described his latest dreams or ventures. The people that where close to Walt were those who lived with him, and his ideas, or both.

On July 13, 1925, Walt married one of his first employees, Lillian Bounds, in Lewiston, Idaho. Later on they would be blessed with two daughters, Diane and Sharon . Three years after Walt and Lilly wed, Walt created a new animated character, Mickey Mouse.

His talents were first used in a silent cartoon entitled Plane Crazy. However, before the cartoon could be released, sound was introduced upon the motion picture industry. Thus, Mickey Mouse made his screen debut in Steamboat Willie, the world's first synchronized sound cartoon, which premiered at the Colony Theater in New York on November 18, 1928.

On December 21, 1937, Snow White and the Seven Dwarfs, the first full-length animated musical feature, premiered at the Carthay Theater in Los Angeles. The film produced at the unheard cost of $1,499,000 during the depths of the Depression, the film is still considered one of the great feats and imperishable monuments of the motion picture industry. During the next five years, Walt

Disney Studios completed other full-length animated classics such as Pinocchio, Fantasia, Dumbo, and Bambi. Walt's drive to perfect the art of animation was endless. Technicolor was introduced to animation during the production of his Silly Symphonies Cartoon Features. Walt Disney held the patent for Technicolor for two years, allowing him to make the only color cartoons. In 1932, the production entitled Flowers and Trees won Walt the first of his studio's Academy Awards. In 1937, he released The Old Mill, the first short subject to utilize the multi-plane camera technique.

Walt rarely showed emotion, though he did have a temper that would blow over as it blew up. At home, he was affectionate and understanding. He gave love by being interested, involved, and always there for his family and friends. Walt's daughter, Diane Disney Miller, once said:

Daddy never missed a father's function no matter how I discounted it. I'd say, "Oh, Daddy, you don't need to come. It's just some stupid thing." But he'd always be there, on time.

Probably the most painful time of Walt's private life, was the accidental death of his mother in 1938. After the great success of Snow White and the Seven Dwarfs, Walt and Roy bought their parents, Elias and Flora Disney, a home close to the studios. Less than a month later Flora died of asphyxiation caused by a faulty furnace in the new home. The terrible guilt of this haunted Walt for the rest of his life.

In 1940, construction was completed on the Burbank Studio, and Disney's staff swelled to more than 1,000 artists, animators, story men, and technicians. Although, because of World War II 94 percent of the Disney facilities were engaged in special government work, including the production of training and propaganda films for the armed services, as well as health films which are still shown through-out the world by the U.S. State Department. The remainder of his efforts were devoted to the production of comedy short subjects, deemed highly essential to civilian and military morale.

Disney's 1945 feature, the musical The Three Caballeros, combined live action with the cartoon animation, a process he used successfully in such other features as Song of the Southand the highly acclaimed Mary Poppins. In all, more than 100 features were produced by his studio.

Walt's inquisitive mind and keen sense for education through entertainment resulted in the award-winning True-Life Adventure series. Through such films as The Living Desert, The Vanishing Prairie, The African Lion, and White Wilderness, Disney brought fascinating insights into the world of wild animals and taught the importance of conserving our nation's outdoor heritage.

Walt Disney's dream of a clean, and organized amusement park, came true, as Disneyland Park opened in 1955. As a fabulous $17-million magic kingdom, soon had increased its investment tenfold, and by the beginning of its second quarter-century, had entertained more than 200 million people, including presidents, kings and queens, and royalty from all over the globe.

Ralph Lauren

Iconic designer Ralph Lauren was born Ralph Lifshitz in New York City on October 14, 1939. Lauren worked in retail at Brooks Brothers before developing a line of neckties. The brand he established, Polo, is now one part of an international empire that includes fragrances, home furnishings, luxury clothing and dining based on a fantasy aesthetic of upper-crust life. Lauren, a funder of cancer research initiatives, has also used his personal fortune to amass a collection of rare and classic cars as well as a massive Colorado ranch.

Ralph Lauren was born Ralph Lifshitz in the Bronx, New York City, on October 14, 1939, the third of four siblings. His parents Frieda and Frank were Ashkenazi Jewish immigrants who had fled Belarus, and the youngster grew up in the Mosholu Parkway area of the family's adopted borough.

At the age of 16, Ralph and his brother Jerry changed their last name to Lauren after having been teased consistently at school. Another brother, Lenny, retained the family name. Ralph was known for his distinctive fashion sense as a teen, finding inspiration in screen icons like Fred Astaire and Cary Grant while having a taste for both classic preppy wear and vintage looks. He went on to attend Baruch College in Manhattan, where he studied business for two years. After a brief stint in the Army, Lauren took on a sales job at Brooks Brothers.

In 1967, while working for Beau Brummell, Lauren began designing his own men's neckties with a wider cut, branding them under the name "Polo" and selling them at large department stores, including Bloomingdale's. Lauren was able to more fully develop his business with a $30,000 loan, eventually expanding his designs to a full menswear line.

In 1970, Lauren was awarded the Coty Award for his men's designs. Following this recognition, he released a line of women's suits tailored in a classic men's style. Then in 1972, Lauren released a short-sleeve cotton shirt in 24 colors. This design, emblazoned with the company's famed logo—that of a polo player, created by tennis pro René Lacoste—became the brand's signature look.

Lauren is known for capitalizing on an aspirational style and key insignia which evokes the British gentry while also referencing the aesthetics of the American upper class. His fashion ideas have been criticized by some for not being particularly innovative while also embraced by scores of consumers who prefer more approachable looks. Lauren subsequently broadened his brand to include a luxury clothing line known as Ralph Lauren Purple, a rough and rustic line of apparel dubbed RRL, a home-furnishing collection called Ralph Lauren Home and a set of fragrances. Polo currently produces clothing for men, women and children and has hundreds of internationally placed stores, including factory stores that produce the majority of his sales domestically.

Lauren has also designed Olympic uniforms for Team USA, though controversy ensued when it was discovered that the competitors' attire for the 2012 summer games was made in China.

During the 1970s Lauren made his foray into the film business as well, further cementing his status as a classic American designer by outfitting cast members for the 1974 film adaptation of The Great Gatsby, starring Robert Redford and Mia Farrow. Lauren also received credit for helping to outfit the cast of 1975's The Wild Party, another early 20th-century outing starring James Coco and Raquel Welch. The designer then became well known for Diane Keaton's rather distinctive looks in the 1977 comedy Annie Hall.

Decades later, Lauren would be enamored by a show that wholeheartedly reflects his particular vision, the PBS series Downton Abbey. He subsequently created a fall collection inspired by the show and sponsored its final season in 2016.

Polo expanded rapidly in the 1980s and 1990s, opening boutiques across the United States and abroad. In 1986, Lauren opened his company's flagship store in New York's Rhinelander Mansion on Madison Avenue, which has since become flanked by several other Lauren stores. With Goldman Sachs having purchased more than a quarter of the company in the mid-'90s, Polo Ralph Lauren went public on June 11, 1997, trading under the symbol RL. As of October 2015, the success of Polo has earned Lauren a personal fortune estimated at more than $6 billion, ranking Lauren among the 200 richest people in the world.

After a year of falling shares, Lauren stepped aside as chief executive of Ralph Lauren Corp. in September 2015 and appointed Stefan Larsson, the global president of The Gap's Old Navy division, to take over as CEO. Lauren took on the role of executive chairman and chief creative officer of the company he founded.

Lauren married teacher and part-time receptionist Ricky Anne Low-Beer in New York City in 1964. The Laurens are the parents of three children: Andrew, David and Dylan. David Lauren is the only one of the three to have made his career at Polo. In 2011 he married Lauren Bush, the niece of President George W. Bush and the granddaughter of President George H.W. Bush. Andrew is a film producer, while Dylan is the owner of the New York City candy store Dylan's Candy Bar.

Lauren had a health scare when he underwent surgery in the mid-1980s to remove a benign tumor from his brain. He has since funded a number of initiatives pertaining to cancer research and care and in 1989 co-founded Georgetown University's Nina Hyde Center for Breast Cancer Research.

Using his considerable fortune, Lauren has amassed a famous collection of rare automobiles, including a 1930 Mercedes-Benz Count Trossi SSK known as "The Black Prince." In 2005, Lauren allowed his collection to be displayed at the Boston Museum of Fine Arts. In 2011, a selection from his car collection was exhibited in Paris.

Kenny Troutt

Kenny A. Troutt was born in 1948 and is the founder of the very celebrated excels communications which can be defined as the teas based Telecommunication Company that utilizes multi-level marketing services to offer out their major products to the targeted audience.

He became one of the richest people on earth during the year 1998 when he sold Teleglobe in which his share was unsettled. But he had to come a very long way to become such a rich person. He is a son of a local bartender. His studies were done in the Illinois University, for which he used to arrange the money by selling insurance to different people. It is because of his hard-work and exertions that now he is involved in horse racing, stock selling and bonds retailing etc.

Though his classmates from school and college wanted to become doctors, teachers or firefighters but Kenny A. Troutt always knew what he wanted to be. Being the oldest among all of his siblings and struggling in the Illinois family, he once told his teacher he wanted to be really rich. And after he surpassed his own childhood dreams, he became the CEO of the Dallas-based Excel Communications Inc. in which his takes in the entire company were around 50% making his net worth more than 1.5 billion dollars.

He came from a very poor family where there were hardly any accommodations in the house; he now owns a 13,000 square foot country French mansion in his name which is just across the street from the manor of Ross Perot. He has had a true experience of hard knocks and the jolts given by the roller coasters of life, he is entirely aware of the ups and downs, high and low roads of life and even though he is always hoping for the best to happen, he still prepares for the worst case scenarios.

He remembers being broke like its yesterday and with his familiarity of living in house projects he still thinks that he is strange to all the wealth that he has earned. He still hears echoes of his father's voice and it because of the fact that he is now one of the most up-and-coming businessmen of the world. He believes in making schemes since this way he has made the most of his negligible resources in getting what he has today, being a part of luminary life.

His life can surely be taken as an example for all those who are in search of the turning point in their lives.

Howard Schultz

Howard Schultz is CEO and chairman of Starbucks, the highly successful coffee company.

"We're not in the business of filling bellies, we're in the business of filling souls."

—Howard Schultz

Born in Brooklyn, New York, on July 19, 1953, Howard Schultz graduated from Northern Michigan University with a bachelor's degree in communications before becoming director of retail operations and marketing for the Starbucks Coffee Company in 1982. After founding the coffee company Il Giornale in 1987, he purchased Starbucks and became CEO and chairman of the company. In 2000, Schultz publicly announced that he was resigning as Starbucks's CEO. Eight years later, however, he returned to head the company. In 2014, Starbucks had more than 21,000 stores worldwide and a market cap of $60 billion.

Howard D. Schultz was born in Brooklyn, New York, on July 19, 1953, and moved with his family to the Bayview Housing projects in Canarsie, a neighborhood in southeastern Brooklyn, when he was 3 years old. Schultz was a natural athlete, leading the basketball courts around his home and the football field at school. He made his escape from Canarsie with a football scholarship to Northern Michigan University in 1970.

After graduating from the university with a Bachelor of Science degree in communication in 1975, Schultz found work as an appliance salesman for Hammarplast, a company that sold European coffee makers in the United States. Rising through the ranks to become director of sales, in the early 1980s, Schultz noticed that he was selling more coffee makers to a small operation in Seattle, Washington, known then as the Starbucks Coffee Tea and Spice Company, than to Macy's. "Every month, every quarter, these numbers were going up, even though Starbucks just had a few stores," Schultz later remembered. "And I said, 'I gotta go up to Seattle.'"

Howard Schultz still distinctly remembers the first time he walked into the original Starbucks in 1981. At that time, Starbucks had only been around for 10 years and didn't exist outside Seattle. The company's original owners, old college buddies Jerry Baldwin and Gordon Bowker and their neighbor, Zev Siegl, had founded Starbucks in 1971. The three friends also came up with the coffee company's ubiquitous mermaid logo.

"When I walked in this store for the first time—I know this sounds really hokey—I knew I was home," Schultz later remembered. "I can't explain it. But I knew I was in a special place, and the product kind of spoke to me." At that time, he added, "I had never had a good cup of coffee. I met the founders of the company, and really heard for the first time the story of great coffee ... I just said, 'God, this is something I've been looking for my whole professional life.'" Little did Schultz know then how fortuitous his introduction to the company would truly be, or that he would have an integral part in creating the modern Starbucks.

A year after meeting with Starbucks' founders, in 1982, Howard Schultz was hired as director of retail operations and marketing for the growing coffee company, which, at the time, only sold coffee beans, not coffee drinks. "My impression of

Howard at that time was that he was a fabulous communicator," co-founder Zev Siegl later remembered. "One to one, he still is."

Early on, Schultz set about making his mark on the company while making Starbucks' mission his own. In 1983, while traveling in Milan, Italy, he was struck by the number of coffee bars he encountered. An idea then occurred to him: Starbucks should sell not just coffee beans but coffee drinks. "I saw something. Not only the romance of coffee, but ... a sense of community. And the connection that people had to coffee—the place and one another," Schultz recalled. "And after a week in Italy, I was so convinced with such unbridled enthusiasm that I couldn't wait to get back to Seattle to talk about the fact that I had seen the future."

Schultz's enthusiasm for opening coffee bars in Starbucks stores, however, wasn't shared by the company's creators. "We said, 'Oh no, that's not for us,'" Siegl remembered. "Throughout the '70s, we served coffee in our store. We even, at one point, had a nice, big espresso machine behind the counter. But we were in the bean business." Nevertheless, Schultz was persistent until, finally, the owners let him establish a coffee bar in a new store that was opening in Seattle. It was an instant success, bringing in hundreds of people per day and introducing a whole new language—the language of the coffeehouse—to Seattle in 1984.

But the success of the coffee bar demonstrated to the original founders that they didn't want to go in the direction Schultz wanted to take them. They didn't want to get big. Disappointed, Schultz left Starbucks in 1985 to open a coffee bar chain of his own, Il Giornale, which quickly garnered success.

Two years later, with the help of investors, Schultz purchased Starbucks, merging Il Giornale with the Seattle company. Subsequently, he became CEO and chairman of Starbucks (known thereafter as the Starbucks Coffee Company). Schultz had to convince investors that Americans would actually shell out high prices for a beverage that they were used to getting for 50 cents. At the time, most Americans didn't know a high-grade coffee bean from a teaspoon of Nescafé instant coffee. In fact, coffee consumption in the United States had been going down since 1962.

In 2000, Schultz publicly announced that he was resigning as Starbucks' CEO. Eight years later, however, he returned to head the company. In a 2009 interview with CBS, Schultz said of Starbucks' mission, "We're not in the business of filling bellies; we're in the business of filling souls."

In 2006, Howard Schultz was ranked No. 359 on Forbes magazine's "Forbes 400" list, which presents the 400 richest individuals in the United States. In 2013, he was ranked No. 311 on the same list, as well as No. 931 on Forbes's list of billionaires around the globe.

Today, no one company sells more coffee drinks to more people in more places than Starbucks. By 2012, Starbucks had grown to encompass more than 17,600 stores in 39 countries around the world, and its market capitalization was valued at $35.6 billion. By 2014, Starbucks had more than 21,000 stores worldwide and a market cap of $60 billion. The incredibly popular coffee company reportedly opens two or three new stores every day and attracts around 60 million customers per week. According to the company's website, Starbucks has been "committed to ethically sourcing and roasting the highest-quality arabica coffee in the world" since 1971.

In March 2013, Schultz made headlines and won wide applause after making a statement in support of the legalization of gay marriage. After a shareholder complained that Starbucks had lost sales due its support for gay marriage (the company had announced its support for a referendum to legalize gay union in the state of Washington), Schultz responded, "Not every decision is an economic decision. Despite the fact that you recite statistics that are narrow in time, we did provide a 38 percent shareholder return over the last year. I don't know how many things you invest in, but I would suspect not many things, companies, products, investments have returned 38 percent over the last 12 months. Having said that, it is not an economic decision to me. The lens in which we are making that decision is through the lens of our people. We employ over 200,000 people in this company, and we want to embrace diversity. Of all kinds." The CEO then added, "If you feel, respectfully, that you can get a higher return than the 38 percent you got last year, it's a free country. You can sell your shares in Starbucks and buy shares in another company. Thank you very much."

Howard Schultz currently resides in Seattle, Washington, with his wife, Sheri (Kersch) Schultz, and two children, Jordan and Addison.

Ken Langone

Kenneth Langone is the founder and CEO of Invemed Associates LLC, a New York Stock Exchange member firm specializing in health care and high technology companies.

He received a B.A. from Bucknell University and an M.B.A. from New York University's Stern School of Business, which he attended at night while working on Wall Street.

The part-time night program was renamed the Langone Program, thanks to the generosity of Mr. Langone and his wife. He currently serves on the Board of Overseers of the Stern School and on the Board of Trustees of New York University, as well as serving as chairman of the Board of Trustees of New York University Medical Center.

In April 2008, the medical center was renamed the NYU Langone Medical Center, reflecting a major gift from the Langones. He was a member of the Bucknell University Board of Trustees for 15 years, where he served as chairman of its Nominating Committee, its Endowment Committee, and as a member of its Executive Committee.

He is a cofounder of the Home Depot and was lead director and member of the Executive Committee of its board from the time Home Depot was founded in 1978 until 2008 when he left the board. He also serves on the boards of Unifi, Inc., Micell Technologies, Relationship Sciences, and Juice Press. Past corporate board memberships include ChoicePoint, Geeknet, General Electric, and YUM

Brands. In addition, he serves on the boards of St. Patrick's Cathedral, the Ronald McDonald House of NY, the Medal of Honor Foundation, the Horatio Alger Society Foundation, and the Harlem Children's Zone and its charter school, the Promise Academy.

Oprah Winfrey

Billionaire Oprah Winfrey is best known for hosting her own internationally popular talk show from 1986 to 2011. She is also an actress, philanthropist, publisher and producer.

"The whole point of being alive is to evolve into the complete person you were intended to be."

—Oprah Winfrey

Oprah Winfrey - Mini Biography (TV-14; 2:58) Watch a mini biography of Oprah Winfrey, who ascended from an impoverished childhood to become one of the most powerful and influential celebrities in the world.

Media giant Oprah Winfrey was born in the rural town of Kosciusko, Mississippi, on January 29, 1954. In 1976, Winfrey moved to Baltimore, where she hosted a hit television chat show, People Are Talking. Afterward, she was recruited by a Chicago TV station to host her own morning show. She later became the host of her own, wildly popular program, The Oprah Winfrey Show, which aired for 25 seasons, from 1986 to 2011. That same year, Winfrey launched her own TV network, the Oprah Winfrey Network.

American television host, actress, producer, philanthropist and entrepreneur Oprah Gail Winfrey was born on January 29, 1954, in Kosciusko, Mississippi. After a troubled adolescence in a small farming community, where she was sexually abused by a number of male relatives and friends of her mother, Vernita, she moved to Nashville to live with her father, Vernon, a barber and businessman. She entered Tennessee State University in 1971 and began working in radio and television broadcasting in Nashville.

In 1976, Oprah Winfrey moved to Baltimore, Maryland, where she hosted the TV chat show People Are Talking. The show became a hit and Winfrey stayed with it for eight years, after which she was recruited by a Chicago TV station to host her own morning show, A.M. Chicago. Her major competitor in the time slot was Phil Donahue. Within several months, Winfrey's open, warm-hearted personal style had won her 100,000 more viewers than Donahue and had taken her show from last place to first in the ratings. Her success led to nationwide fame and a role in Steven Spielberg's 1985 film The Color Purple, for which she was nominated for an Academy Award for Best Supporting Actress.

Winfrey launched the Oprah Winfrey Show in 1986 as a nationally syndicated program. With its placement on 120 channels and an audience of 10 million people, the show grossed $125 million by the end of its first year, of which Winfrey received $30 million. She soon gained ownership of the program from ABC, drawing it under the control of her new production company, Harpo Productions ('Oprah' spelled backwards) and making more and more money from syndication.

In 1994, with talk shows becoming increasingly trashy and exploitative, Winfrey pledged to keep her show free of tabloid topics. Although ratings initially fell, she earned the respect of her viewers and was soon rewarded with an upsurge in popularity. Her projects with Harpo have included the highly rated 1989 TV miniseries, The Women of Brewster Place, which she also starred in. Winfrey also signed a multi-picture contract with Disney. The initial project, 1998's Beloved, based on Pulitzer Prize-winning novel by Toni Morrison and starring Winfrey and Danny Glover, got mixed reviews and generally failed to live up to expectations.

Winfrey, who became almost as well-known for her weight loss efforts as for her talk show, lost an estimated 90 pounds (dropping to her ideal weight of around 150 pounds) and competed in the Marine Corps Marathon in Washington, D.C., in 1995. In the wake of her highly publicized success, Winfrey's personal chef, Rosie Daley, and trainer, Bob Greene, both published best-selling books.

The media giant contributed immensely to the publishing world by launching her "Oprah's Book Club," as part of her talk show. The program propelled many unknown authors to the top of the bestseller lists and gave pleasure reading a new kind of popular prominence.

With the debut in 1999 of Oxygen Media, a company she co-founded that is dedicated to producing cable and Internet programming for women, Winfrey ensured her place in the forefront of the media industry and as one of the most powerful and wealthy people in show business. In 2002, she concluded a deal with the network to air a prime-time complement to her syndicated talk show. Her highly successful monthly, O: The Oprah Magazine debuted in 2000, and in 2004, she signed a new contract to continue The Oprah Winfrey Show through the 2010-11 season. Now syndicated, the show is seen on nearly 212 U.S. stations and in more than 100 countries worldwide.

In 2005, Winfrey helped give The Color Purple a new life onstage as one of the producers of the eleven-time Tony-nominated musical, which ran on Broadway until 2008. A revival of the musical, which Winfrey co-produced in 2015, won the Tony Award for best revival of a musical.

In 2009, Oprah Winfrey announced that she would be ending her program when her contract with ABC ended, in 2011. Soon after, she moved to her own network, the Oprah Winfrey Network, a joint venture with Discovery Communications.

Despite a financially rocky start, the network made headlines in January 2013, when it aired an interview between Winfrey and Lance Armstrong, the American cyclist and seven-time Tour de France winner who was stripped of his seven Tour titles in 2012 due to doping charges. During the interview, Armstrong admitted to using performance-enhancing substances throughout his cycling career, including the hormones cortisone, testosterone and erythropoietin (also known as EPO). "I am deeply flawed ... and I'm paying the price for it, and I think that's okay. I deserve this," he stated. The interview reportedly brought in millions of dollars in revenue for OWN.

Of her interview with Armstrong, Winfrey said in a statement, "He did not come clean in the manner I expected. It was surprising to me. I would say that, for myself, my team, all of us in the room, we were mesmerized by some of his answers. I felt he was thorough. He was serious. He certainly prepared himself for this moment. I would say he met the moment. At the end of it, we both were pretty exhausted."

In March 2015, Winfrey announced that her Chicago-based Harpo Studios would close at the end of the year to consolidate the company's production operations to the Los Angeles-based OWN headquarters. Winfrey's television empire was launched at the studio and it had been home to her daily syndicated talk show through its finale in 2011. "The time had come to downsize this part of the business and to move forward. It will be sad to say goodbye," said Winfrey, "but I look ahead with such a knowing that what the future holds is even more than I can see."

Winfrey returned to acting in Greenleaf, which marked her first recurring scripted television role. The original family drama revolves around a Memphis megachurch and premiered on OWN in June 2016.

According to Forbes magazine, Oprah was the richest African American of the 20th century and the world's only Black billionaire for three years running. Life magazine hailed her as the most influential woman of her generation. In 2005, Business Week named her the greatest Black philanthropist in American history. Oprah's Angel Network has raised more than $51,000,000 for charitable programs, including girls' education in South Africa and relief to the victims of Hurricane Katrina.

Winfrey is a dedicated activist for children's rights; in 1994, President Clinton signed a bill into law that Winfrey had proposed to Congress, creating a nationwide database of convicted child abusers. She founded the Family for Better Lives foundation and also contributes to her alma mater, Tennessee State University. In September 2002, Oprah was named the first recipient of the Academy of Television Arts & Sciences' Bob Hope Humanitarian Award.

Winfrey campaigned for Democratic presidential hopeful Barack Obama in December 2007, attracting the largest crowds of the primary season to that point. Winfrey joined Obama for a series of rallies in the early primary/caucus states of Iowa, New Hampshire, and South Carolina. It was the first time Winfrey had ever campaigned for a political candidate.

The biggest event was at the University of South Carolina football stadium, where 29,000 supporters attended a rally that had been switched from an 18,000-seat basketball arena to satisfy public demand.

"Dr. (Martin Luther) King dreamed the dream. But we don't have to just dream the dream anymore," Oprah told the crowd. "We get to vote that dream into reality by supporting a man who knows not just who we are, but who we can be." The power of Winfrey's political endorsement was unclear (Obama won Iowa and South Carolina, but lost New Hampshire). But she has a clear track record of turning unknown authors into blockbuster best-sellers when she mentions their books on her program.

After The Oprah Winfrey Show ended on September 9, 2011, Oprah has remained in the rapidly shifting and converging media field through The Oprah Winfrey Network (OWN), which launched on January 1, 2011.

In her final season of her talk show, Oprah made ratings soar when she revealed a family secret: she has a half-sister named Patricia. Oprah's mother gave birth to a baby girl in 1963. At the time, Oprah was 9 years old, and living with her father. Lee put the child up for adoption because she believed that she wouldn't be able to get off public assistance if she had another child to care for. Patricia lived in a series of foster homes until she was 7 years old.

Patricia tried to connect with her birth mother through her adoption agency after she became an adult, but Lee did not want to meet her. After doing some research, she approached a niece of Winfrey's, and the two had DNA tests done, which proved they were related.

Winfrey only learned of her sister's existence a few months before she made the decision to publicize the knowledge. "It was one of the greatest surprises of my life," Winfrey said on her show.

In November 2013, Winfrey received the nation's highest civilian honor, the Presidential Medal of Freedom. President Barack Obama gave her this award for her contributions to her country.

Winfrey has been in a relationship with Stedman Graham, a public relations executive, since the mid-1980s. They became engaged in 1992, but never tied the knot. The couple lives in Chicago, and Winfrey also has homes in Montecito, California, Rolling Prairie, Indiana, and Telluride, Colorado.

Shahid Khan

Shahid Khan, an illustrious Pakistani-American businessman, is a manufacturer of automobile parts Flex-N-Gate in Illinois, and the owner of Jacksonville Jaguars of the National Football League.

Born on 18 July, 1950, in Lahore, Khan moved to the United States at the age of 16 with dreams in his eyes. He wanted to be an architect. Khan knew that one has to work to turn your dreams into reality, and towards this end, he washed dishes in restaurants at the rate of $1.20 per hour to pay for his expenses.

He did his graduation in B.Sc with Industrial Engineering from UIUC College of Engineering in 1971. Khan finally became a US citizen in 1991.

Even while Khan was studying at the University of Illinois, he had embarked on his path towards realizing his dreams. His first career stint was with Flex-N-Gate. Soon after graduation, Khan got selected for the post of Engineering Director of the company.

He was the pioneer of Bumper Works; this division specialized in making car bumpers for customized pickup trucks and body shop repairs. Ambition together with perseverance is a formidable combination! Khan first endeavored to own an NFL team in 2010.

An agreement was entered upon to acquire 60 percent of St. Louis Rams. However, the minority shareholder, Stan Kroenke, put a spoke in the wheel, by exercising a clause in his ownership and the agreement was nullified. Not one to put down his weapons, Khan agreed to purchase the Jacksonville Jaguars from Wayne Weavers, following the approval of NFL in 2011.

Finally, the deal materialized in the same year, and the sale was finally completed in 2012. Khan is presently on the board of the NFL Foundation. Khan's thirst for success was boundless, and in 2013, he once again started negotiations to purchase the London Soccer Club Fulham. The deal was finalized in the same year, but the purchase price was kept confidential.

Having bought Flex-N-Gate in 1980, Khan, in a period of just nine years, made his company the only supplier for the entire Toyota line in the United States. In 2012, Forbes magazine featured him on its front cover. Khan symbolises what is known as "the face of the American Dream". It is worth mentioning here that Khan was the first member of an ethnic minority ever to own an NFL team!

Khan married his college sweetheart Ann Khan in 1977. They had met for the first time at the college bar and had forged an everlasting bond. Married for 31 long happy years, the dashing couple is blessed with two children, Tony and Shanna.

In 2011, the title of "Lincoln Laureate" was bestowed on him by the Lincoln Academy of Illinois for his philanthropic work in the state.

Kirk Kerkorian

American financier Kirk Kerkorian (born 1917) parlayed a charter flight business consisting of a single $5,000 plane into one of the world's great fortunes. In 2007, Kerkorian ranked number 26 on the Forbes magazine list of the 400 richest Americans, with assets estimated at $9 billion.

Kerkorian's activities made headlines because, although his personal lifestyle was far from flamboyant, he made deals in high-profile industries: movies, Las Vegas hotels, and most recently automobile manufacturing. Sometimes stereotyped as a purely financial animal who stripped industries of their profits in his quest for ever-greater wealth, Kerkorian was a generous man who by one estimate gave away some 20 percent of his enormous fortune to charity. One of the most noteworthy aspects of Kerkorian's career was its longevity. As he approached his ninetieth year he shunned geriatric activities in favor of a widely publicized bid to increase his influence over General Motors, the world's largest automaker.

"When you're a self-made man you start very early in life," Kerkorian told K.J. Evans of the Las Vegas Review-Journal in one of his rare interviews (reproduced on the website The First 100 Persons Who Shaped Southern Nevada). "In my case it was at nine years old when I started bringing income into the family. You get a drive that's a little different, maybe a little stronger, than somebody who inherited." He was born Kerkor Kerkorian on June 6, 1917, to Ahron and Lily Kerkorian, Armenian immigrants who had settled in California's San Joaquin Valley farming region. The youngest of four children, he spoke Armenian at home, learning English on the streets and during his intermittent schooling.

Ahron Kerkorian, almost illiterate, was a watermelon and raisin farmer who aimed toward higher things; he bought several farms and amassed land holdings of 1,000 acres. But he lost them all during a recession in 1921 when banks foreclosed on his mortgages. The family ran into severe financial difficulties and was forced to move some 20 times, with Kerkorian helping bring in money as a newsboy and as a watermelon dealer in one of the city's produce markets. He spent more time out of school than in it, often getting into minor scrapes as a member of a neighborhood street gang. Kerkorian was sent to a disciplinary school and declared his education over after finishing eighth grade; he was 16 years old.

Applying lessons from learned from street fights, Kerkorian began training as a boxer with his older brother Nishon. At 20 he won his first fight by decision and went on to a Pacific amateur welterweight championship and a record of 33 wins and 4 losses, earning the nickname "Rifle Right." But Kerkorian soon found another activity that he enjoyed even more than boxing, after a friend with whom he worked installing furnaces took him on a ride in a single-engine airplane. Enthralled but lacking the money for the expensive hobby, he showed up at the Happy Bottom ranch of the celebrity female pilot Florence "Pancho" Barnes and proposed that he take on heavy barn duties, including milking cows and shoveling manure, for payment in flying lessons. The aviatrix agreed, and a flying instructor at the ranch helped Kerkorian get a letter stating, spuriously, that he had completed high school in Los Angeles.

That qualified Kerkorian to enter the military, but instead he spent World War II in a more profitable though no less hazardous position, as a civilian employee of Britain's Royal Air Force, flying Mosquito bombers from Canada, where they were built, to Scotland. The planes were easily destabilized by ice on the wings during their northerly crossing, and often dumped their pilots into the freezing North Atlantic. Kerkorian once ran out of gas just as the clouds parted to reveal his airstrip in Scotland, and glided in. He made 33 bomber deliveries for the R.A.F. and banked most of his generous earnings of $1,000 per run.

Back in Los Angeles in the summer of 1945, Kerkorian bought a single-engine Cessna plane for $5,000, planning to give flying lessons and operate an occasional charter service. The charter end of the business soon occupied most of his attention as he prospered by offering flights between Los Angeles and fast-growing Las Vegas, Nevada. Kerkorian began spending more and more time in the gambling capital, often gravitating toward the craps tables and gaining a reputation as unflappable even as he won or lost tens of thousands of dollars. He purchased Los Angeles Air Service, a small charter airline, and renamed it Trans International Airlines (TIA) in 1947. In buying and selling used planes he often emerged with healthy profits, and at one point he became the first entrepreneur to offer charter jet service. Married briefly once before, he met his second wife, showgirl Jean Maree Hardy, in Las Vegas. The pair had two daughters, Tracy and Linda, whose names inspired that of Kerkorian's holding company, Tracinda Corporation.

In 1962 Kerkorian made his first million dollars by selling TIA to the automaker Studebaker, investing most of it in an 80-acre plot of land near the growing Las Vegas strip. In 1965 he repurchased TIA and offered stock in the company for sale through a Fresno stockbroker of Armenian ancestry. These two decisions together raised Kerkorian from successful entrepreneur to tycoon. After he made another deal that joined his plot of land to the Strip itself, he leased it to the owners of what became the Caesar's Palace hotel and collected $4 million in rent before selling the land outright for $5 million more. After TIA's stock rose from $9.75 a share to $32, Kerkorian sold the company to the Transamerica Corporation in 1968, netting $85 million in Transamerica stock.

Kerkorian once again plowed his profits back into new enterprises, opening the International Hotel in 1969 and pioneering the idea of Las Vegas as a family vacation destination instead of an illicit adult playground. The hotel had a "youth hostel" kids' activities area and offered family tours to nearby attractions such as Lake Mead. Kerkorian offered stock in the hotel's parent company, International Leisure. He had to sell some of his own stock in order to pay heavy European gambling debts, and he eventually gave up gambling completely. In 1970 he sold the International, as well as the Flamingo Hotel, which he had turned into an unofficial employee training ground for the swank new International, to the Hilton hotel chain.

By that time, Kerkorian had begun what Money magazine termed "an epic Hollywood-Wall Street romance": his ongoing relationship with the MGM film studios. Borrowing $42 million from European banks, he wrested control of the company from its existing large stockholders in 1969 with an outlay of about $650 million. He opened the MGM Grand Hotel in Las Vegas in 1973. The MGM studio did not prosper artistically during the period of Kerkorian's leadership, but his financial wizardry was unimpeded. He acquired the United Artists studio for $380 million, formed the conglomerate MGM/UA, and sold the new entity to cable television magnate Ted Turner in 1985 for $1.5 billion. Turner ran into financial problems in the late 1980s, and Kerkorian obligingly repurchased the company for $780 million, selling it once again to controversial Italian financier Giancarlo Parretti for $1.3 billion in 1990. Parretti, under investigation by European financial authorities, submitted in turn to a Kerkorian buyback, whereupon Kerkorian finally cashed out with a $2.9 billion sale to Sony in 2004.

Two things were noteworthy about this financial odyssey. The first was that upon Kerkorian's departure, MGM was in much the same financially shaky condition as it was when he acquired it; he did not succeed in creating a global colossus like Turner's CNN. And second, even as he pocketed billions, Kerkorian was legendary for his refusal to accept free passes to MGM-owned movie theaters; he lined up and bought tickets along with other patrons. He acquired a Beverly Hills mansion but lived alone in its small guest house. Kerkorian acquired a reputation as a recluse, but he was regularly seen in Los Angeles and Las Vegas restaurants and bars, wielding a $10,000 bankroll and preferring cash to credit cards. After his second marriage dissolved, he dated several actresses and then married tennis star Lisa Bonder in 1999 after living with her for several years. In 2002 the marriage broke up and spawned a divorce and paternity suit in which Bonder asked for $320,000 a month in alimony and child support. In nonmarital matters he was generous without dispute; he gave hundreds of millions of dollars to charities, particularly in Armenia.

During the last stages of his involvement with MGM, Kerkorian turned to a larger industry still. In 1990 he began buying shares in the Chrysler Corporation, performing a variety of maneuvers designed to increase the value of the company's stock, and in 1994 he and former Chrysler chairman Lee Iacocca launched a hostile takeover of the company. Their plan was beaten back, but Kerkorian reaped billions in profits from several Chrysler stock buybacks. A $5 billion windfall from Chrysler's incorporation into German automaker Daimler-Benz in 1998 was not enough for Kerkorian, who filed suit (unsuccessfully) against the company for misrepresenting the new DaimlerChrysler entity as a merger of equals; chairman Juergen Schrempp, in comments made in 2000, characterized it instead as a takeover, which would have resulted in additional profits for stockholders.

In 2005 Kerkorian set his sights still higher. He acquired a 9.9 percent stake in General Motors and seated one of his representatives on the company's board, then urged GM to investigate a merger with the already existing partnership of French automaker Renault and Japan's Nissan. Press reports at the time suggested that Kerkorian envisioned high-flying Nissan head Carlos Ghosn as GM's new chairman. These efforts, too, were beaten back by GM's existing management in 2006—with difficulty, for Kerkorian's net worth by this time amounted to more than half of GM's total market valuation of some $16.4 billion. In November of 2006 Kerkorian's Tracinda Corp. sold most of its GM stock.

An inspiration to senior citizens everywhere, Kerkorian made his high finance automotive transactions while he was in his late 80s. He reportedly jogged every morning, and friends reported that his tennis game was improving. Still frugal in his personal habits, he allowed himself the luxury of $150 haircuts for his still-thick mane of gray hair. In an era when finance was increasingly the province of young movers and shakers with advanced degrees, he was a self-made man who outperformed competitors one-third his age.

John Paul DeJoria

John Paul Jones DeJoria is an entrepreneur and philanthropist; who is well known for his Paul Mitchell hair products. He is also the co-founder and Chief Executive Officer of The Patron Spirits Company. The billionaire has a net worth of $4 billion.

DeJoria was born on 13th April 1944 in Echo Park, Los Angeles, California. His parents got divorced when he was two and at nine years of age he was selling newspapers and cards in order to support his family. DeJoria attended Atwater Elementary and then John Marshall High School. His mother could not support both her children so she had to send them to a foster home. As a teenager he got involved in some street gang activities but he decided to change his path after being advised by a teacher at school. In 1962 after he graduated from high school, he joined the Navy where he spent two years.

To make ends meet DeJoria did many jobs including being a janitor to selling insurance. He got a job at Redken Laboratories and this was the beginning of his entrepreneurial success. He was eventually fired from this job after a disagreement over some of the business policies. He co-founded John Paul Mitchell Systems with the hairdresser Paul Mitchell in 1980. He took a loan of 700 dollars for the start-up. John Paul DeJoria also owns seventy percent of The Patrons Spirits Company which is a world famous tequila brand. He co-founded the company in 1989. It sold more than 2,450,000 cases in 2011. He is also a founding member of the nightclub chain House of Blues and has interests in Ultimat Vodka, Pyrat Rum, Sun King Solar, Solar Utility, Three Star Energy, Touchstone Natural Gas, Diamond Audio, ROK AMERICAS, John Paul Pet, a diamond company, J&D Acquisitions LLC, Larson's parent company, Triumph, Striper, a Harley-Davidson dealership, Carver and Marquis Yachts.

John Paul DeJoria is also an actor and producer in the film industry. He made an appearance in the 2008 comedy movie 'You Don't Mess with the Zohan' and in 'The Big Tease' in which he played his former business partner Paul Mitchell. He also made an appearance in the season two of the TV series 'Weeds'. He also acted and narrated in the television commercial of Patron in 2011. In 2012 he displayed his support of Captain Paul Watson of the Sea Shepherd Conservation Society through a video release. DeJoria also supports Food4Africa. He joined Nelson Mandela in Africa to help feed more than seventeen thousand orphan children. His company Paul Mitchell also provided food for more than 400000 poor children.

This once homeless billionaire is today inducted in the esteemed Horatio Alger Association of Distinguished Americans. His rule of life is 'Success unshared is failure' and this policy can be seen throughout his company. His employees are very happy to work with him. He has maintained such a friendly work environment and paychecks far more than what the market normally offers.

Today the hero of this 'rags to riches story' has come a long way. He lives with his wife and six children in their Austin home.

Do Won Chang

All you need to do to make it big is to dream big and work on them. Do Won Chang, owner of celebrated clothing brand <u>Forever 21</u> is a living proof. From a single store in Los Angeles to 457 stores in nearly fifty countries today, Do Won Chang's story is referred to time and again by aspiring businessmen all over the world.

Do Won Chang originally belongs to South Korea. He never had a big life in his own country either. In fact, he grew up working in coffee shops. When Chang immigrated to the United States with his wife Jin Sook Chang, he knew he wanted to do some kind of business. He decided upon retail when he saw the businessmen driving swankiest cars in town. This was the sole reason he took up the garment business, as stated in many interviews.

Fashion 21 was the name they first chose for the small store that the couple started off in Highland Park, Los Angeles in the year 1984. Thanks to Chang's extreme dedication, business grew steadily. In the very first year, it made a $700,000. It expanded further in the United States and outside. The couple changed the brand name to Forever 21 later. Ever since, the name has been expanding aggressively, now with stores in a whole of 50 countries around the world.

Won Chang's purpose of entering the garment business – earn a lot of money, has been served. But it was not without lot of efforts and perseverance that he attained the pedestal. Chang is often heard saying that success comes only when there is enough understanding of the business and the legal culture that is involved in it. And success is slow. "Success isn't a dash race, it's a marathon" he says.

Apart from being a devoted and aggressive businessman, he is also a very spiritually inclined person. Chang is an ardent believer in Christianity, which is the reason why the verse 'John 3:16' is inscribed on every Forever 21 bag. He also does a lot of charity work with churches all over the world. Bible, he says is his favourite book.

Do Won Chang is also known to be very attached to his family. When it comes to business, family is what he trusts. While he owns stores along with his wife, his daughters Linda and Esther are also involved in the business. While Linda takes care of the marketing, Esther takes care of the visual elements like the graphics and the window display of the stores.

With a very unusual success story behind him, Do Won Chang is an inspiration for thousands of other immigrants from Asia who come every day to United States with big dreams to live up to.

Francois Pinault

François Pinault, (born Aug. 21, 1936, Champs Géraux, Côtes-du-Nord, France), French businessman and art collector who created a retail empire, especially noted for its luxury goods.

Pinault's earliest jobs were with his father's timber company; in 1963 he founded Société Pinault, a timber and building materials firm (reorganized as Pinault SA in 1988).

Pinault acquired department store Au Printemps SA in 1992, and, after purchasing mail-order company La Redoute, he formed Pinault-Printemps-Redoute in 1994 (renamed PPR in 2005).

Working through his holding company, Artémis SA (founded in 1992), he added a wide range of firms. Pinault's purchase of a nearly 30 percent stake in British auction house Christie's in 1998 signaled his shift toward expensive brands—and affirmed his interest in art.

After acquiring 42 percent of luxury-goods retailer Gucci Group NV in 1992, Pinault transformed it into a luxury-brand conglomerate, and in 2004 he gained a controlling stake. His American holdings included Samsonite luggage and a ski resort in Vail, Colo.

Pinault was also an avid art collector, and by the early 21st century he had acquired some 3,000 works. After efforts to build a museum in France failed, Pinault in 2005 bought the Palazzo Grassi in Venice, and the following year he began displaying a small percentage of his collection—including works by Cindy Sherman and Jeff Koons—at the villa.

In 2007 Pinault and the Palazzo Grassi were selected to create a contemporary art museum at the Punta della Dogana, an unused Venetian customs house on the Grand Canal.

The museum, with an interior designed by Japanese architect Ando Tadao, opened in 2009 and housed a number of works from Pinault's collection.

Leonardo Del Vecchio

Ranking 71st on the Forbes global fortune list, Leonardo Del Vecchio is the second wealthiest man in Italy. He is the president and founder of the world's leading company in the development, production marketing and distribution of glasses. The company is none other than Luxottica. They make their own glasses and are world leaders in the eye glasses industry. The self-made successful business man, Leonardo Del Vecchio boasts a net worth of $11 billion.

Leonardo was born to a poor Milanese family in 1935. Leading a fatherless childhood, he was forced to live in an orphanage at the age of 7 under the care of nuns and at the age of 14, circumstances required him to work in order to support his impoverished family. His first job was in Milan working as a novice with a tool manufacturer. He joined evening classes studying industrial engineering at the age of 19, continuing working during the day all along.

With time Leonardo became fascinated and much passionate about glasses and frame and this drove him into moving to a small village in Venice known as Agordo, where one can find all the players of the eye glass industry offering a lot to learn about the trade from design to marketing.

In 1967, Leonardo took the decision to enter the glasses assembly business. He now had 6 years of experience but it was not easy due to fierce competition.

Expanding his work, Leonardo found his own company, Luxottica. Ten years later in 1976, Luxottica stopped making frames for other brands and launched its own eye wear brand. Using extensive research, the brand went on to become the market leader. There was no looking back; Leonardo's effective strategies helped him in developing a successful sales network.

Leonardo's futuristic approach, timely decisions and strategies helped Luxottica to have full control and take over every stage of the eye glass manufacturing process. The Luxottica group now also began acquisitions in areas of distribution and retail. The group eventually took over some of the most famous Italian brands such as Lens Crafters, Persol and Vogue moving on to acquiring Ray Ban, the most famous American brand. Over the years, Luxottica has been seen to acquire all major eye glass brands including Oakley which was bought for $2.1 billion, giving Luxottica a major break in the sports segment. In addition to this, Luxottica now manufactures for the world famous brands such as Versace, Ralph Lauren, DKNY, Ferragamo, Prada, Chanel and Armani.

George Soros

George Soros is a self-made billionaire known for his investment savvy and his vast body of philanthropic work.

Born in Budapest, Hungary, on August 12, 1930, George Soros survived Nazi occupation followed by Communist-rule in Hungary in the mid-1940s and emigrated to London. There he studied economics and after earning his degree, moved to New York City in 1956, where he entered a life of finance. He began his renowned philanthropic efforts in 1979, and as of 2012 his lifetime giving amounts to more than $7 billion via his Open Society Foundations.

George Soros was born Gyorgy Schwartz in Budapest, Hungary, on August 12, 1930 to parents Tividar and Erzebat Schwartz. To avoid growing anti-Semite persecution, his father changed their surname to Soros in 1936. As a teenager, he survived the Nazi invasion and occupation of Hungary in 1944. A few years after WWII ended, Soros emigrated from the then-Communist-dominated Hungary in 1947 and made his way to England. There, at the London School of Economics, Soros began studying Karl Popper's The Open Society and Its Enemies, which explores the philosophy of science and serves as Popper's critique of totalitarianism. The essential lesson the book imparted to Soros was that no ideology owns the truth, and that societies can flourish only when they operate freely and openly and maintain respect for individual rights—thoughts that would deeply influence Soros for the rest of his life.

Soros graduated in 1952, and in September 1956 he sailed to New York and took a job at Wall Street brokerage firm F.M. Mayer. After working for a few more firms, in 1973 Soros set up his own hedge fund (the Soros Fund, soon after renamed the Quantum Fund and later the Quantum Fund Endowment) with $12 million from investors. The fund, with Soros at the helm, found massive success through its various iterations, and as of September 2015, Soros, at 85 years of age, was deemed as the 21st richest person in the world, with an estimated net worth of $26 billion.

George Soros began his philanthropic activity in 1979, and he established the Open Society Foundations in 1984. The foundations fund a range of global initiatives "to advance justice, education, public health, business development and independent media." The causes Soros helps with his foundations are numerous (the foundations' list of activities goes on for 500 pages), but they include aiding in regions struck by natural disaster, establishing after-school programs in New York City, funding the arts, lending financial assistance to the Russian university system, fighting disease and combating "brain drain" in Eastern Europe.

While a towering figure in the philanthropic world, George Soros is also a provocative figure. Among his controversial positions are that he supports altering the United States' "war on drugs" to avoid the current extent of criminalization, he was involved in and profited heavily from the U.K. currency crisis of 1992 (dubbed Black Wednesday), he has written several books on the looming collapse of the financial markets (and certain observers accuse him of manipulating the markets to reach his ends) and he has said that policies of the United States and Israel have given rise to global anti-Semitism.

Controversial or beloved, with his countless organizations (through which he shapes public policy and undertakes vast humanitarian projects), financial empire and the 12 books he's written on subjects ranging from the war on terror to global capitalism, George Soros is an influential figure and a giant in finance and the realm of philanthropy.

Soros has five children and has been divorced twice. He married his third wife, Tamiko Bolton, in 2013.

Li Ka-shing

Li Ka-shing, a Hong Kong entrepreneur and philanthropist, is one of the wealthiest persons in Asia. A very powerful figure in his own country, he is also one of the most influential businessmen in the entire Asian subcontinent. He was the Chairman of the Board of the now defunct Hutchison Whampoa Limited (HWL) and currently serves as the Chairman of Cheung Kong Holdings, one of Hong Kong's leading multi-national conglomerates. He has businesses involved in diverse fields such as real estate, ports, electricity, telecommunication and internet. The story of his phenomenal success is truly an inspiring one. Born to poor parents in mainland China, he fled to Hong Kong as a refugee after Japanese invasions in 1940. He also lost his father at a young age and was forced to take up a job at the age of 15. An intelligent, hard working and determined boy, he went on to form his own businesses in the ensuing years and rose to become one of Hong Kong's leading industrialists. Respected all over the world as a man truly committed to ethics and moral values, Ka-shing is also a noted philanthropist and has donated over a billion dollars to charity. Despite being one of the richest individuals in the world, he is known for being an unassuming person who leads a frugal lifestyle.

Li Ka-shing was born in Chaozhou in Guangdong province, China, on 29 July 1928. His family was of modest means and his father, a teacher, headed a local primary school.

He grew up in a period of great political turmoil in China. His family fled to Hong Kong in 1940 after the Japanese invasion of China. The family struggled to re-establish their lives in their new surroundings when another major tragedy befell the family within a span of three years. His father became ill with tuberculosis and died a painful death when Li Ka-shing was just 15 years old.

He was forced to drop out of school and take up a job in order to provide for his family. He started working in a plastics trading company as a salesman selling plastic watchbands and belts. He worked hard, often working up to 16 hours a day and proved to be a capable salesman.

After gaining valuable experience working in plastic industries, Li was able to form his own business, a plastics company named Cheung Kong in 1950. Initially the company manufactured artificial flowers and exported them to the United States. Throughout the 1950s the company saw steady growth and Li began looking for opportunities to expand the business.

He purchased his first factory in 1958; this would be the first of his many real estate investments. Over the ensuing years he changed the focus of his plastics company which he eventually transformed into a property development and management company.

The business thrived over the following years and the company was renamed Cheung Kong Holdings in 1971. It was listed on the Hong Kong Stock Exchange in 1972.

He expanded his business by acquiring Hutchison Whampoa from HSBC in 1979. This added multiple diverse industries to his existing business. He soon transformed Hutchison into the world's largest independent operator of ports, with investments in container port facilities around the world, including in Hong Kong, Canada, China, the United Kingdom, Rotterdam, Panama, Bahamas and many others.

Li also forayed into the technology business. One of his firms, Horizons Ventures, an investment and venture capital firm, which specifically backs new internet and technology startup firms, bought a stake in doubleTwist, a digital . He also has a 0.8% stake in social networking website Facebook which he acquired through his other firm, Li Ka Shing Foundation. He also has a stake in Ginger Software Incorporated.

Li Ka-shing founded Cheung Kong Industries in 1950s as a plastics manufacturer. The company eventually expanded and diversified into various other fields and evolved into Cheung Kong (Holdings) Limited in the 1970s. It is today one of Hong Kong's leading multi-national conglomerates which operates in over 50 countries and employs over 240,000 staff worldwide.

Harold Simmons

Harold C. Simmons beat his tennis pro for the first time last week, and his back is paying the price.

Mr. Simmons, his shirt collar open and tieless, repeatedly readjusts himself in his office chair, sometimes propping his feet atop his large desk. Green blips periodically flash on the darkened computer screen behind him. Neatly arranged on the desk are a hand-held calculator, a yellow legal pad and a few personal items.

Mr. Simmons' boyish "Huck Finn' looks belie his 58 years and the successful high-rolling investment record that strikes fear in the hearts of corporate managements from giants GAF, Lockheed and Chrysler to smaller Ben E. Keith, a beer distributor company that Mr. Simmons courted in the early 1980s.

"In the last 10 years, I have acquired and managed successfully some substantial companies,' the soft-spoken Mr. Simmons said. "It (once) was easy for management to say, "Here is a raider who simply wants to come in and buy the company to destroy the company.' They can't say that now.'

Mr. Simmons lacks the flash usually associated with an investment strategist whose personal worth is conservatively estimated at $1.75 billion and whose companies total nearly $7 billion in assets.

Privately, he prefers the casualness of dirt bike racing, tennis, horseback riding and flying his private jet to the precisely coiffed hair and buttoned-down meticulousness of a Wall Street raider. His haunts are far from the Wall Street jungle, at homes in Dallas, Aspen, Colo., and Santa Barbara, Calif.

Professionally, he is fiercely dedicated to making money in innovative ways -- a passion that has led to his being characterized as anti-union and hostile to corporate managements.

He's a quick learner, conducts no-nonsense meetings and asks incisive questions after already having thought an issue through, say associates. "He's not a desk pounder,' says Hugh Shurtleff of T.I.M.E.-D.C., a Lubbock trucking company that Mr. Simmons bought and liquidated in the late 1970s when the company's union workers refused to take wage concessions.

"He knew nothing about the trucking business, but before that day was over, I think he knew what made us as a business tick, what deregulation would do, what Teamsters control would mean,' said Mr. Shurtleff, recalling Mr. Simmons' initial trip to visit the company.

"That is difficult to do,' said Mr. Shurtleff, who now works for another Simmons holding called Sybra Inc. "He's successful because he is analytical, able to see what may happen down the line.'

Mr. Simmons does not denounce the corporate raider tag, but bristles at the suggestion that he dismantles corporations and managements with reckless abandon: "I buy companies without being invited to . . . . That's the definition of a raider.

"But they can't say I am a destructive person because they simply can't find any facts to support that position,' Mr. Simmons said. "Both the companies and the shareholders have prospered greatly as the result of my entry into a situation.'

"The facts justify my great reputation," Mr. Simmons said, smiling wryly.

An organizational chart of Mr. Simmons' vast financial network fans out from Contran Corp., a family trust whose sole trustee is Mr. Simmons. Beneath Contran and held in various interlinked ownerships is Dallas-based Valhi Inc., a $2.2 billion publicly traded company that has been Mr. Simmons' principal investment arm. Valhi, which earned $85.9 million last year, is trading at about 17 1/2 a share, or about 20 times earnings.

Beneath Valhi are other publicly traded companies -- Houston-based NL Industries, Baroid Corp. and Sybra -- the hands and fingers for many of Mr. Simmons' major investment and takeover deals.

But Mr. Simmons' companies also are generally strong businesses with global reach:

*NL Industries is a major maker of titanium dioxide pigment and specialty resins, producing over $1 billion in sales and operating income of $251.8 million in 1988.

*Baroid, an oil and gas industry services company, posted operating income of $30.6 million on sales of $494 million in 1988.

Two other wholly owned Valhi companies, Medford Corp. and Medite Corp. operate in the forest-products industry. The forest-products operation generated $212 million in sales and operating income of $30.3 million in 1988. Sybra operates Arby's fast food restaurants in about seven states and produced $9.8 million of operating income on revenue of $81 million in 1988. Valhi's hardware division, a $59 million revenue operation, produced operating income of $7.6 million in last year.

Keystone Consolidated Industries, a steel rod and wire manufacturer run by Mr. Simmons older brother, Glenn, has been an exception to the earnings pattern. The company has been hurt by labor problems and eroding markets since it was acquired in 1981. In recent months, the sale of certain assets and cost cutting have begun to improve its financial outlook.

Mr. Simmons' career has been a mix of takeovers and well-timed investments. Some deals have verged on "greenmail,' a common tactic where an investor amasses substantial holdings in a company with the intent of forcing management to pay large settlements to halt the assault.

As a result of stalking PSA Inc., the now-defunct San Diego-based airline, Mr. Simmons more than doubled his investment to make a $17.7 million profit between 1978 and 1982.

A 17 percent stake in GAF in 1983 paid him $197.9 million, a $139.9 million gain in three years. And a $218 million investment in Sea-Land Corp. in 1985 gave him an $83 million profit 11 months later. He doubled a $5 million investment made in Ozark Airlines in late 1980 by early 1981.

He bought Amalgamated Sugar in 1982 for $35 million, then sold off its unprofitable Amalgamize Division for about $30 million. He held onto the rest of the company, which has churned out profits of at least $25 million every year since.

His savvy surfaced in the 1986 acquisition of NL Industries, a petroleum and chemical company. NL's former management had offered to buy back a significant portion of its shares to discourage an unsolicited takeover.

Noticing that more shareholders had offered to tender their shares than NL's management had expected, Mr. Simmons recognized the company's vulnerability and seized the opportunity.

He acquired enough NL shares to trigger anti-takeover measures called a poison pill, which allowed stockholders to tender their shares back to the company. Far more stockholders sold their shares than expected. Another provision of the poison pill left the company virtually helpless to seek outside help. Within days, Mr. Simmons sued, won and took control of the company.

More recently, his 10 percent investment in Lockheed has fueled rumors about his intent. Mr. Simmons says only that his Lockheed stake is just an investment at this time.

"I am not interested in buying Lockheed at higher prices,' said Mr. Simmons. "This will probably turn out to be a very long-term investment.'

These days, Mr. Simmons is eyeing Georgia Gulf Corp., an Atlanta chemical company whose financial successes made it a perfect Simmons target. It posted a profit of $193.6 million on revenue of $1.06 billion last year, has virtually no debt, strong cash flow, and is in a low profile industry that does not attract intense takeover attention.

Georgia Gulf's management holds about 18 percent of the stock and had talked openly about acquiring other companies with its cache of cash. Mr. Simmons said the inside ownership probably dissuaded others from mounting a hostile bid.

Through NL Industries, Mr. Simmons began accumulating Georgia Gulf's common stock. When the Georgia Gulf board failed to listen to Mr. Simmons' offer to participate in a $55-a-share plan, NL threatened to oust the board -- a chess move that forced Georgia Gulf to sit down and entertain various transactions.

Mr. Simmons said he would give Georgia Gulf time to work out a plan -- about two weeks at the most. If the plan meets with Mr. Simmons approval, he will sell his stock as part of the shareholder transaction. But if they "hesitate or come up with the wrong solution that does not provide value . . . we will continue our solicitation-and-tender offer.'

That is the cat-and-mouse game of wills that Mr. Simmons plays so well. He likes to call the other person's bluff without putting up money -- preferring to step inside another's defense rather than launch an overpriced and expensive external assault on management.

"In today's environment, the highest bidder gets a company,' said Mr. Simmons. "But we felt that the results would be the same (in the Georgia Gulf case) . . . That remains an option and we would probably pursue that as the next option.'

When news of his 9.9 percent holdings in Georgia Gulf drove up the stock price to around $59 a share, Mr. Simmons dropped his share to 8.9 percent, a 230,000 share selloff. News of the sale sent the price back to the low $50-a-share range.

Before the dust could settle, Mr. Simmons purchased 230,000 shares for between $52 and $53 a share, transactions that turned a $7-a-share profit and restored 9.9 percent stake in Georgia Gulf. Arbitragers -- investors who circle and acquire stock on the speculation that merger activity will inflate its value -- may not have been as lucky. At least Mr. Simmons hopes they weren't.

"I think I taught the arbs a lesson,' he says. "The arbs are my enemies,' said Mr. Simmons his voice becoming more animated.

"The arbs jump, raise expectations of prices and make it more difficult for me to buy stock at a price that makes sense for me . . . . I am always in a running battle with the arbs. I try to confuse them, to use them, to take advantage of them and give them a pretty clear message that the stock is too high, and I am going to sell it.'

"I think I am different from many raiders in that they set their sights on a target, and they want to buy 5 percent, 10 percent of a company and make a offer for the whole company with the idea that someone will buy the whole company and that they make a profit on their stock,' said Mr. Simmons. "Basically, I am a buyer or a seller depending on what the price is.'

For Mr. Simmons, the morning perusal of the financial pages is often the start of a financial investment that will move markets a few weeks later. If a company mentioned in a financial publication attracts his interest, Mr. Simmons will obtain its financial statements and crunch numbers.

Sometimes he will review analyst reports or conduct his own analysis of the industry in which the company does business. He never talks to the analysts or to the company directly, lest that contact generate unbridled speculation or defensive tactics from management.

"I am a very simple person,' said Mr. Simmons. "I can read the numbers, the financial statements and can add and subtract . . . . I just have enough confidence in the judgment I can make from the public information . . . . You can get too much information and can get lost in the woods.'

"(But) It's not a risk-free business when you buy from outside; you are always taking a chance because you are not buying complete information . . . . We always have surprises. You just hope that good ones offset the bad ones." Sometimes he will quickly make the decision to buy. Other times, he will simply compile cold statistics for years before making a decision. He generally goes after one target at a time, unlike some corporate raiders who may have several irons in the fire. And his targets tend to be in narrow manufacturing industries, rather than service or high-tech industries.

"Basically, the service company does not provide the numbers I like,' Mr. Simmons said. "Many service companies are very successful. If they are very succesful, they are selling at prices higher than I would like to pay."

Mr. Simmons' remains a staunch supporter of former Drexel Burnham Lambert junk bond king Michael Milken, a friend and occasional tennis companion. He says he believes Mr. Milken has been "hounded' unfairly by the government and the press and that "the junk bond market has been hurt by his absence."

Mr. Simmons said he opposes efforts to restrict the use of junk bonds, contending that the market will correct its own foibles more effectively than government intervention. Some may pay too much and incur massive interest and principal payments on debt-financed takeovers. But the prudent will dance and the foolhardy will stumble, he contends.

"Wall Street always does everything to excess, fee-driven deals, pay too much for acquisitions,' said Mr. Simmons. "(But) the market is going to go on as long as things make business sense."

"(The market) is seeing some losses, but that is what the market is all about."

Mr. Simmons also believes regulations requiring investors in public companies to disclose holdings of more than 5 percent stock ownership in a company serves to further entrench management by sending them an early warning signal. Said Mr. Simmons, "I think every investor should buy stock based on their own interpretations of the values, not on what I am doing. What I am doing is my own proprietary business."

Former SMU business dean Roy Herberger recalls conversations with Mr. Simmons about business subjects as diverse as Japanese influence in U.S. financial markets to the West German economy.

"Every conversation I have had with him I have come away with something to read,' said Mr. Herberger. "He is a consummate deal maker, and an academician in analyzing a situation."

Harold Clark Simmons' life has been punctuated by two failed marriages and controversial business ventures early in his career that left him close to broke and in legal trouble.

The son of two schoolteachers, he grew up in Golden, a small rural community about 80 miles east of Dallas. After high school, he attended the University of Texas "because my father said I should go to college.' His father wanted him to be a lawyer, but his rural background attracted him to study agriculture.

He made the Longhorn basketball team and was graduated with bachelor's and master's degrees in economics. His master's thesis: An Economic Analysis of Agricultural Policies and Programs as Proposed by Leading Texas Farm Journals.

Mr. Simmons couldn't find a job in his field of study. He "discovered the only job available was secretary of agriculture,' he muses. "So, I had to get into something else."

He took a job as an investigator for the U.S. Civil Service Commission, but left to work for the Federal Deposit Insurance Corp., and then for the former Republic National Bank of Dallas as a junior loan officer.

Realizing that the only way he was going to make a lot of money was to go into business for himself, Mr. Simmons sank $5,000 in cash and took a $95,000 bank loan to buy a small pharmacy across the street from Southern Methodist University.

At that time, Dallas business executive James J. Ling -- the L in LTV Corp. -- had launched an acquisition pace that made LTV a major conglomerate. Mr. Ling's style fascinated Mr. Simmons. In the scaled-down footsteps of Mr. Ling, Mr. Simmons launched an acquisition binge that brought him drugstores around the state. Some were acquired through hostile takeovers.

Mr. Simmons sold his stores in 1973 to Jack Eckerd Corp. for $50 million in the drugstore chain's common stock. But within two years, the paper value of the stock had fallen, slicing the value of his Eckerd holdings to about $12 million.

A brief dip into financial services and insurance almost financially ruined him.

Mr. Simmons had used stock from his finance company to prop up the value of an insurance company he owned. When the finance company failed, the insurance company also fell, and federal officials accused him of mail fraud and various securities violations.

Mr. Simmons was cleared of all charges, but the experience made a deep impression on him. Though dampened, his desire to be an entrepreneur, was not doused. The lesson he learned is that he would have to do a better job of looking out for his own well-being. Mr. Simmons was put to the test two other times: First, while fending off his second wife's attempt to break the family trust that controlled Contran during a messy divorce battle; then, in repelling a hostile bid from Mr. Ling to take over Contran in the late 1970s.

Mr. Ling -- the man who Mr. Simmons said he admired and had hired to help revive Mr. Simmons businesses -- launched a hostile bid for control of Contran, the company that controlled his fortune. Mr. Simmons won the battle, bought out Mr. Ling, and took Contran private. Both Mr. Simmons and Mr. Ling describe that skirmish as "just business."

"Contran was like any business transaction, we were trying to get the very best values for the shareholders,' Mr. Ling said recently. "This idea of him as a raider tag is nonsense, for the birds. That's just cry-baby talk."

"I ascribe 100 percent . . . . that there is no question that he is creating value for shareholders," said Mr. Ling.

In recent years, Mr. Simmons' behind-the-scenes philantrophy has become more public. A charitable foundation run by his daughter Lisa contributes about $1.3 million a year to various cultural arts, homeless shelters and juvenile intervention programs.

The largest contributions have been to medical research. Mr. Simmons, who suffers discomfort from a mild form of arthritis, became familiar with the work done by the University of Texas Southwestern Medical Center through his doctor.

Satisfied that it was a "high quality operation and a worthwhile cause," Mr. Simmons began financially aiding the center.

In 1982, he pledged $8 million over 10 years to support basic research into the causes of inflammatory arthritis, particularly those affecting the spine. The gift made it possible for UT Southwestern to double the number of faculty members specializing in arthritis research, but also meant that the research staff had outgrown its home.

In 1988, he contributed $12 million more as part of a $41 million gift to the school, the contribution is believed to be the largest single gift ever made to a Texas school. About $24 million will be devoted to cancer research; $12 million for arthritis research and $5 million to construct a building for cancer research. The $24 million for cancer will fund a Comprehensive Cancer Center that will do specialized research. Four endowed specialized research chairs will be named for Mr. Simmons' four daughters. Another chair for breast cancer research will be named for Annette, his wife.

His name is on the Harold C. Simmons Arthritis Research Center and the proposed Simmons Biomedical research building will honor his mother and father. He also has contributed $1.9 million to establish a chair in marketing at SMU's Edwin L. Cox School of Business.

"I think at this point in his life, he has thought long and hard about how he could use his money to help others,' said Kern Wildenthal, president of the Southwestern Medical Center. "His approach is to identify the people he will entrust with his money and stay out of the way.'

Larry Ellison

Larry Ellison is the founder and CEO of Oracle Corporation, which earned him a spot as fifth wealthiest person in the world in 2014.

Larry Ellison was born in the Bronx, New York, on August 17, 1944, to single mother Florence Spellman. When he was nine months old, Ellison came down with pneumonia, and his mother sent him to Chicago to be raised by her aunt and uncle, Lillian and Louis Ellison, who adopted the baby.

After high school, Ellison enrolled at the University of Illinois, Champaign (1962), where he was named science student of the year. During his second year, his adopted mother died, and Ellison dropped out of college. The following fall, he enrolled at the University of Chicago, but he dropped out after only one semester.

Ellison then packed his bags for Berkeley, California, with little money, and for the next decade he moved from job to job at such places as Wells Fargo and Amdahl Corporation. Between college and his various jobs, Ellison had picked up basic computer skills, and he was finally able to put them to use as a programmer at Amdahl, where he worked on the first IBM-compatible mainframe system.

In 1977, Ellison and two of his Amdahl colleagues founded Software Development Labs and soon had a contract to build a database-management system—which they called Oracle—for the CIA. The company had fewer than 10 employees and revenue of less than $1 million per year, but in 1981, IBM signed on to use Oracle, and the company's sales doubled every year for the next seven years. Ellison soon renamed the company after its best-selling product.

In 1986, Oracle Corporation held its IPO (initial public offering), but some accounting issues helped wipe out the majority of the company's market capitalization and Oracle teetered on the brink of bankruptcy. After a management shakeup and a product-cycle refresh, however, Oracle's new products took the industry by storm, and by 1992 the company was the leader in the database-management realm.

Success continued, and as Ellison was Oracle's largest shareholder, he became one of the wealthiest people in the world. Ellison set his sights on growth through acquisitions, and over the next several years he gobbled up several companies, including PeopleSoft, Siebel Systems and Sun Microsystems, all of which helped Oracle reach a market cap of roughly $185 billion with some 130,000 employees by 2014.

When he's not busy bolstering his software empire, Ellison races yachts (his yacht Rising Sun is over 450 feet long—one of the largest privately owned vessels in the world), and in 2010 he joined the BMW Oracle racing team and won the prestigious America's Cup. The victory brought the cup to the United States for the first time in 15 years, a win the team repeated in 2013.

Jim Carrey

Jim Carrey is a comedian and actor best known for comedic and dramatic film roles in movies including Ace Ventura: Pet Detective and The Truman Show.

Comedian and actor Jim Carrey was born in Newmarket, Ontario, Canada, on January 17, 1962. Carrey relocated to Los Angeles to pursue comedy, eventually landing a spot on the sketch comedy show In Living Color. He went on to huge box office success in comedies, including Ace Ventura: Pet Detective and The Mask, and delivered acclaimed dramatic performances in The Truman Show and Man on the Moon. Recent films include Kick Ass 2 (2013) and Dumb and Dumber To (2014).

Actor and comedian James Eugene Carrey was born on January 17, 1962, in Newmarket, Ontario, Canada. Carrey got his start with a spot doing stand-up at a Toronto comedy club when he was just 15 years old. By 1979, he had left the factory job as a janitor he had taken in 1978 to help support his family and was making his living as the opening act for successful comics Buddy Hackett and Rodney Dangerfield.

In 1983, Carrey headed west to Hollywood where he starred in a made-for-television movie called Introducing...Janet. Carrey's appearances on TV in programs such as The Duck Factory and Jim Carrey's Unnatural Act (1991) led to a regular role on the hit comedy In Living Color.

Carrey's big screen debut came with 1984's Finders Keepers, but he didn't find success until he played the titular role in the 1994 comedy Ace Ventura: Pet

Detective. From there, Carrey's expressive face, expert mimicry skills and physical brand of comedy kept the hits coming. He followed with The Mask (1994), Dumb and Dumber (1994), Ace Ventura: When Nature Calls (1995), Batman Forever (1995), The Cable Guy (1996) and Liar Liar (1997).

Carrey took a successful dramatic turn as Truman Burbank in Peter Weir's The Truman Show (1998), for which he won a Golden Globe award for Best Actor. He teamed up with legendary director Milos Forman for the Andy Kaufman biopic Man on the Moon (1999), co-starring Courtney Love. For his dead-on portrayal of Kaufman, Carrey took home his second Golden Globe. Despite his Golden Globe success, he didn't earn a nomination for an Academy Award. Carrey has become one of the highest-paid actors in Hollywood, with an reported asking price of $20 million.

In the summer of 2000, Carrey portrayed a character with two dueling personalities (both in love with the same woman) in the comedy Me, Myself and Irene. That fall, wearing pounds of green fur and makeup, he starred as the titular curmudgeon in the long-awaited big budget film version of Dr. Seuss' holiday classic, How the Grinch Stole Christmas, directed by Ron Howard. In 2003, the actor starred as a man endowed with God-like powers in Bruce Almighty with Jennifer Aniston. The following year, Carrey starred opposite Kate Winslet in Charlie Kaufman's Eternal Sunshine of the Spotless Mind.

Carrey continued to take on a variety of comedic roles, starring such films as Fun with Dick and Jane (2005), A Christmas Carol (2009) and Mr. Popper's Penguins (2011). He also enjoyed supporting parts in The Incredible Burt Wonderstone (2013) with Steve Carell and Kick Ass 2 (2013). In 2014, Carrey reteamed with Jeff Daniels for Dumb and Dumber To.

Carrey has a daughter, Jane, from his marriage to Melissa Womer (from 1987 to 1995). He was married briefly to Dumb & Dumber co-star Lauren Holly before entering a yearlong romance with his Me, Myself and Irene leading lady, Renee Zellweger. He was later involved with actress/model Jenny McCarthy.

Mariah Carey

With hits such as "Vision of Love" and "I Don't Wanna Cry," pop diva Mariah Carey holds the record for most No. 1 debuts in Billboard Hot 100 history.

"Never, never listen to anybody that try to discourage you."

—Mariah Carey

Mariah Carey - Mini Biography (TV-MA; 3:50) A short biography of Mariah Carey who is one of the top-selling artists of all time. The Grammy award winner rose to fame with her 1990 album "Vision of Love" and made a comeback with "The Emancipation of Mimi" in 2005.

Mariah Carey was born March 27, 1970, in Huntington, Long Island, New York, and began taking voice lessons at age four. At 18 she signed with Columbia records, and her first album had four No. 1 singles, including "Vision of Love" and "I Don't Wanna Cry." She went on to produce several more albums (later with other studios) and top singles, and is one of the best-selling female artists of all time.

Singer Mariah Carey was born March 27, 1970, in Huntington, Long Island, New York, to Alfred Roy Carey, a Venezuelan aeronautical engineer; and Patricia Carey, a voice coach and opera singer. Has two older siblings: a brother, Morgan, and a sister, Alison. Carey is known as one of the top "pop divas" of the 1990s, having sold more than 80 million albums worldwide. Her voice spans more than five octaves and she writes most of her own music.

Carey's parents divorced when she was 3 years old. She stunned her mother by imitating her operatic singing as early as age two, and was given singing lessons starting at age four. After graduating in 1987 from Harborfields High School in Greenlawn, New York, Carey moved to Manhattan where she worked as a waitress, coat check girl, and studied cosmetology while writing songs and actively pursuing a music career at night.

When she was 18 years old, Carey and her friend, singer Brenda K. Starr, went to a party hosted by CBS Records. Starr convinced Carey to bring along one of her demo tapes. She intended to give the tape to Columbia's Jerry Greenberg, but Tommy Mottola, the president of Columbia Records (later Sony), intercepted it before she could hand it to Greenberg. After listening to the tape on the way home from the party, Mottola signed Carey immediately and set her to work on her first album, Mariah Carey (1990) which included four No. 1 singles: "Vision of Love," "Love Takes Time," "Some Day," and "I Don't Wanna Cry." Her second album Emotions was released in 1992; the title track became her fifth No. 1 single, and included hits "Can't Let Go" and "Make it Happen."

In March 1992, Carey appeared on MTV's Unplugged. This performance was released as an album and a home video, resulting in another No. 1 single (a cover of The Jacksons' "I'll Be There"). Her next album Music Box (1993) cut back a bit on the lavish studio production techniques heard in her previous albums, and included the No. 1 singles, "Dreamlover" and "Hero." Her November 1994 release

Merry Christmas combined traditional Christian hymns with new songs. In 1995 she released Daydream; the first single "Fantasy" debuted at No. 1. It also included collaborations with R&B and hip-hop artists, such as Wu-Tang Clan and Boyz II Men ("One Sweet Day").

Her 1997 album, Butterfly, included 11 compositions written by Carey, and demonstrated her continued interest in hip-hop and R&B, including the Sean "Puffy" Combs-produced "Honey," her 12th No. 1 hit. Carey's 1998 album, #1's, featured her 13 previous chart-topping singles as well as the Academy Award-nominated "The Prince of Egypt (When You Believe)," a duet with fellow pop diva Whitney Houston.

In July 2001, Carey was admitted into a New York-area hospital and put under psychiatric care after suffering what her publicists called a "physical and emotional collapse." Carey had been preparing to promote her upcoming feature film debut, Glitter, and its accompanying soundtrack album, but cancelled all public appearances. The release of Glitter was subsequently pushed back from late August to late September 2001. Carey was released from the hospital after two weeks.

In January 2002, Carey and EMI (the corporate owner of Virgin Records, with whom Carey had signed a reported $80 million contract in April 2001) severed their relationship. Though the film and soundtrack for Glitter failed to generate the desired box office and sales totals, Carey reportedly walked away from Virgin with nearly $50 million as part of her severance agreement. In May 2002, she signed a deal with Universal Music Group's Island/Def Jam Records. In December 2002, Carey staged a comeback with her eighth album, Charmbracelet, which debuted in third place on the charts. The record's accompanying tour, her first in more than three years, launched in June 2003.

In 2012, Carey was chosen as a new judge for season 12 of the popular FOX television show American Idol, taking a seat alongside Randy Jackson, Nicki Minaj and Keith Urban.

Carey has sold around 160 million albums worldwide. She is the third best-selling female artist of all time, according to the Recording Industry Association of America. With 2008's Touch My Body (from her eleventh studio album $E=MC^2$), Carey passed Elvis Presley to become second only to the Beatles for the most No. 1 hit singles in the United States.

Outside of her music career, Carey is active in fundraising for The Fresh Air Fund, a nonprofit agency that provides free summer vacations to disadvantaged children in New York City.

In January 2015, Carey inked a deal to become the latest diva songstress to take up residency in Las Vegas beginning in May.

In June 1993, Carey married Mottola in a spectacular ceremony at Manhattan's St. Thomas Episcopal Church. The couple divorced in 1998. Carey then dated Latin singer Luis Miguel for three years, but their relationship reportedly ended in the summer of 2001.

Carey married rapper/actor/talent show host Nick Cannon on April 30, 2008, in a secret ceremony in the Bahamas. The couple had been dating for less than two months, their romance having blossomed after he appeared in her music video for "Bye Bye." In 2011, Carey and Cannon welcomed twins Moroccan and Monroe. After six years of marriage, in August 2014, the couple announced their separation. It was also reported that a confidentiality agreement was issued that bars discussing the details of their split publicly. In January 2015, it was reported that Cannon officially filed for divorce.

In January 2016, Carey became engaged to Australian businessman James Packer in New York City, but in October of that year, it was announced that the couple had split.

Frank O'Dea

Frank O'Dea is an example of what can be achieved when there is hope of a tomorrow, a vision of a better life, and resources to take action.

It's a classic rags-to-riches story Frank O'Dea never tires of telling and audiences worldwide are unceasingly inspired by. O'Dea's name, probably not as recognizable as The Second Cup, the cutting-edge coffee shop franchise business he co-founded, is a Canadian of extraordinary courage, overcoming life obstacles that might well have deterred a person of lesser faith. Prior to Christmas (2008), O'Dea told his story to some four-hundred community and business leaders gathered for The Salvation Army's inaugural Hope in the City Leadership Breakfast in downtown Toronto

Born Francis O'Dea in 1945 of a loving Montreal family of high moral and life values, Frank should have found an easy path to manhood. But that was not to be. He was sexually abused as a young boy; little wonder, some say, alcohol became an all-too-familiar companion in his teens and threatened to destroy his life and that of his family. That's why Frank's father took a "tough love" stance, ordering his son to leave home with no family contact until he straightened himself out.

In his recently published memoir, When All You Have Is Hope, O'Dea says he always had hope. "Without hope you perish," he told the morning audience. In his years as a self-described panhandler, O'Dea's definition of hope was 99 cents to buy a drink, a place to sleep near his adopted home—a park bench, or The Salvation Army's Harbour light Centre at Jarvis and Shuter Streets where Frank spent more than one cold night.

After The Salvation Army, Frank found another helping hand, a Toronto paint store retailer who gave him a job for five dollars a day stocking shelves and cleaning up ... if he showed up. One of the days he did show for work, the store radio played an announcement for an alcohol treatment program. It was the beginning of the rest of his life.

Earning a thousand bucks from selling coin sorters to churches, O'Dea was well on his way to becoming the man Sir Paul McCarty, Kofi Annan, Colin Powell, the Governor General and scores of high-power celebrities recognize as a friend and man of vision and heart.

Hope, vision and action represent O'Dea's business plan for just about every project he tackles from getting sober in the 1970's to starting a coffee shop at the Scarborough Town Centre that grew to six, then a hundred shops across Canada. Hope, he says, gives you reason to carry on to the next day. Vision enables you see possibilities others don't. Action is the natural force and direction that follows from vision.

The sale of The Second Cup business to Cara Operations Limited, an international food services company, left Frank with great wealth and an inspirational story of overcoming great personal obstacles, opening doors to the highest political and corporate movers and shakers. O'Dea is quick to state he is an example of what can be achieved, even by a lone, down-and-out individual begging for wine money on city streets, when there is hope of a tomorrow, a vision of a better life, and resources to take action.

There's another happy ending to the Frank O'Dea story. He did eventually reconcile with his family and credits his father for having saved his life—forcing him to face up to denial that had plagued his life.

Suze Orman

Suze Orman is a financial adviser best known for her television appearances on The Suze Orman Show, and for her best-selling self-help financial planning books.

"My job is to be the financial truth crusader. ...Hope for the best. But plan for the worst."

—Suze Orman

Suze Orman was born in Chicago, Illinois, on June 5, 1951. Orman started out as a financial adviser at Merrill Lynch, founding the successful Suze Orman Financial Group in 1987. Orman then began writing popular guides to finance and appeared in several PBS specials based on her work. In 2002, she began taping The Suze Orman Show on CNBC, while continuing to publish bestsellers regularly.

Susan Lynn Orman was born on June 5, 1951, in Chicago, Illinois. With her books, television show, and other media efforts, Suze Orman has established herself as one of the top personal finance experts in the United States. "My job is to be the financial truth crusader. ...Hope for the best. But plan for the worst," Orman explained to People magazine.

Her life had a less-than-auspicious start, however. The youngest of three children, she struggled to overcome a speech impediment. Her family also wrestled with financial challenges. After high school, Orman went to the University of Illinois at Urbana-Champaign. There she majored in social work, but left in 1973 before completing her degree. Buying a van, Orman set out to see America with some friends. She ended up in Berkeley, California, where she eventually landed a waitressing job at the Buttercup Bakery. During her seven years at the bakery, Orman pursued a dream of opening up her own restaurant. She shared her dream with one of her longtime customers, Fred Hasbrook, and he gave her a check for $2,000 in 1980. Hasbrook also approached other customers to contribute to Orman, and she ended up with $50,000 for her restaurant venture.

Knowing little about money management or investing, Orman sought help from a representative at Merrill Lynch. She met with a broker, and put her money into an account there. Although she had told him that she only made $400 a week and needed to keep her money safe, the broker chose to pursue the risky strategy of buying options. He told that she could make "a quick $100 a week" and had her sign a blank form giving him control over her funds. The plan worked well at first, but she ended up losing all of her money within three months.

Meanwhile, Orman had been trying to learn as much about investing as she could. She read the Wall Street Journal and Barron's, and she tuned in to the PBS financial series Wall Street Week. After losing all her money, Orman decided to become a broker and applied to the same Merrill Lynch office where she had lost her earlier investment. The company hired her "to fill their women's quota," Orman explained to Publisher's Weekly. She was told that women weren't meant to work this business and that she would be gone in six months.

During her training, Orman discovered that her broker had violated the company's policies. She sued the company, and Merrill Lynch eventually settled with her out of court. Orman studied hard to learn about all sorts of investing opportunities, and she did well for her customers. In 1983, she left to join another firm as a vice president. Orman started her own firm in 1987.

Orman got her first media exposure through a local radio station after writing to complain about another guest that provided incorrect information on an investment product. "The next Saturday I went down there and did a show. After that, my phone started to ring off the hook," Orman told Success magazine. Soon Orman became a guest expert for other radio and television programs.

In 1995, Orman had her first book, You've Earned It, Don't Lose It, published. She went on an extensive tour to promote the work, which eventually sold 700,000 copies. Two years later, Orman hit the best-sellers list with The 9 Steps to Financial Freedom. The book, based on a workshop that she gave, sold more than 3 million copies. "It was at that point that I made the change from being a financial adviser who wanted simply to give a book to my clients to a No.1 New York Times best-selling author," Orman told People magazine.

Orman's career continued on its upward trajectory with 1999's The Courage to Be Rich. That same year, she was named one of Money magazine's "Power Brokers." More popular titles soon followed, including 2001's The Road to Wealth and 2003's The Laws of Money, The Lessons of Life. She also became a hit on public television with a number of financial specials based on her books.

In 2003, Orman received accolades for her television series, The Suze Orman Show. Her show won a Gracie Allen Award from the American Women in Radio and Television organization in the National/Network/Syndicated Talk Show category. The following year, Orman won a Daytime Emmy Award for Outstanding Service Show Host for the The Laws of Money, The Lessons of Life special. She went on to win the 2005 Gracie Allen Award for Outstanding Program Host—a feat she repeated in 2006, 2007, 2008, and 2009. She also won a second Daytime Emmy Award in 2006 for Outstanding Service Show Host for The Money Show for the Young Fabulous & Broke.

In addition to her numerous awards, Orman has received critical praise for her work. A critic for Entertainment Weekly wrote "Suze has managed to do for money what Trading Spaces did for design and Top Chef did for food—make it accessible and entertaining."

Orman did, however, come under fire for not predicting the recent economic downturn. She told U.S. News & World Report that she "believed the CEOs that went on television...and told everyone it was going to be OK, that they were fine." Orman indicated that the crisis was a wake-up call for many. "Our problems were that we were spending money that we never had," she said. She also faced criticism for her business relationships with the brokerage firm TD Ameritrade and credit reporting company Fair Isaacs.

Once a waitress earning $400 a month, Orman has become a nationally known personality. She has even been spoofed several times on the popular late night comedy series Saturday Night Live. Orman loves Kristen Wiig's impression of her, calling it the "greatest honor of my career."

Besides her own weekly television program, Orman makes appearances on other programs, such as The Oprah Winfrey Show and The Today Show. She also writes a regular advice column for O magazine. Outside of her work, Orman supports a number of charities and has been known to help out her fans with free financial advice and other forms of support.

Orman and her partner Kathy Travis have been together since 2001. They divide their time between homes in New York, Florida, and San Francisco.

Leonardo DiCaprio

Oscar-winning American actor Leonardo DiCaprio has starred in such features as 'Titanic,' 'The Aviator,' 'Blood Diamond' and 'The Wolf of Wall Street.'

"I loved imitating people ... I loved joking around with my parents and creating different characters. I liked doing my own little homemade skits."

—Leonardo DiCaprio

Leonardo DiCaprio - Romeo + Juliet (TV-14; 2:37) Leonardo DiCaprio was so intent on getting the role of Romeo that he paid his own way to fly to Australia to meet with director Baz Luhrmann.

Born in 1974 in Los Angeles, California, Leonardo DiCaprio is an actor known for his edgy, unconventional roles. He started out in television before moving on to film, scoring an Oscar nomination for his role in What's Eating Gilbert Grape (1993). In 1997, DiCaprio starred in James Cameron's epic drama Titanic, which made him a huge star. The actor has also paired up with iconic director Martin Scorsese for several projects, including The Aviator (2004) and The Departed (2006). His more recent films include Inception (2010), Django Unchained (2012), The Wolf of Wall Street (2013) and The Revenant (2015), winning his first Oscar for the latter.

Born on November 11, 1974, in Los Angeles, California, Leonardo Wilhelm DiCaprio is the only child of Irmelin and George DiCaprio. His parents divorced when he was still a toddler. DiCaprio was mostly raised by his mother, a legal secretary born in Germany.

Despite his parents' early divorce, Leonardo DiCaprio remained close to his father, a comic book artist and distributor. With his parents' urging, Leonardo explored his creative side, developing an early interest in acting. "I loved imitating people ... I loved joking around with my parents and creating different characters. I liked doing my own little homemade skits," DiCaprio told Back Stage. But he didn't have much success in Hollywood until he reached his early teens.

For years, DiCaprio had trouble landing an agent. One agent even recommended DiCaprio change his name to Lenny Williams to improve his appeal. By the early 1990s, however, the burgeoning actor began landing regular television work. His early credits included guest appearances on such programs as The New Lassie and Roseanne. He also landed a role on the dramatic comedy Parenthood. While the show proved to be short lived, DiCaprio reportedly met fellow actor Tobey Maguire while making the series. The two have remained good friends ever since.

In 1991, DiCaprio took a leap forward when he was cast as a semi-regular on the family comedy Growing Pains, with Kirk Cameron and Alan Thicke. He made his film debut in the low-budget horror flick Critters 3 that same year. But DiCaprio really first demonstrated his talents as a serious actor two years later. Proving to the critics that he was more than a just good-looking teenager, DiCaprio starred opposite Robert De Niro in This Boy's Life. The film delved into the difficult relationship between a young boy and his abusive stepfather in this adaptation of Tobias Wolff's memoir. DiCaprio impressed critics, holding his own on screen up against acting heavyweight De Niro.

DiCaprio turned heads again with his performance in What's Eating Gilbert Grape? (1993), co-starring Johnny Depp. His portrayal of a child with mental disabilities earned him an Academy Award nomination for best supporting actor. The accolades he received from this film solidified DiCaprio's reputation as talent to watch out for.

DiCaprio continued to pursue interesting and diverse film projects: He starred in the 1995 coming-of-age drama The Basketball Diaries, and worked with Russell Crowe, Sharon Stone and Gene Hackman on the western The Quick and the Dead that same year. In Romeo + Juliet (1996), Baz Luhrmann's modern retelling of William Shakespeare's tragic love story, DiCaprio played Romeo to Claire Danes's Juliet.

It was another tragic love story that helped propel DiCaprio's career to a new level in 1997. He co-starred with Kate Winslet in James Cameron's Titanic, the turn-of-the-century story about the sinking of the titular ocean liner. In the film he plays Jack, a poor artist who falls for the rich and beautiful Rose (Winslet) on board. The couple faces danger not only from Rose's fiancé (Billy Zane), but the ship itself after it strikes an iceberg. The film's production budget topped more than $200 million, and was, at the time, the most expensive film ever made.

Titanic became both a critical and commercial smash hit. It garnered 14 Academy Award nominations and won 11, taking home such distinctive honors as best picture and best director. It was the first film to reach the billion dollar mark in international sales.

The success of the film also showed that DiCaprio could handle traditional Hollywood leading man roles. He quickly became a world-famous celebrity with a growing following of admirers, his charm and youthful good looks landing him on People magazine's list of the "50 Most Beautiful People" in 1997 and 1998.

After Titanic, DiCaprio had a bit of a career slump, as The Man in the Iron Mask (1998) and The Beach (2000) proved to be disappointments both financially and artistically. However, DiCaprio soon bounced back. He demonstrated his range as an actor in two noteworthy features from 2002, Steven Spielberg's Catch Me if You Can and Gangs of New York. The latter film served as the first of many projects DiCaprio would work on with famed director Martin Scorsese.

In Scorsese's The Aviator (2004), DiCaprio took on the challenge of playing one of America's most famous businessmen, receiving another Academy Award nomination for his portrayal of the eccentric and reclusive Howard Hughes. In 2006, he starred in a pair of well-received films, Blood Diamond and The Departed. DiCaprio earned his third Academy Award nomination for Blood Diamond, a dramatic thriller about the pursuit of a precious gem in war-torn Sierra Leone. For the compelling Scorsese-directed crime saga The Departed, he co-starred with Matt Damon and Jack Nicholson.

In 2008, DiCaprio reunited with Winslet in Revolutionary Road, a tense film about a 1950s suburban couple facing a myriad of personal problems. He explored a fantastical future in Christopher Nolan's Inception (2010), where technology allows people to invade the dreams of others. That same year, DiCaprio starred in the Scorsese thriller Shutter Island.

DiCaprio took on another famous figure in the 2011 biographical drama J. Edgar. Directed by Clint Eastwood, the film explores the life of J. Edgar Hoover, who ran the FBI for nearly five decades. To prepare for the role, DiCaprio conducted extensive research, and visited many of Hoover's haunts in Washington, D.C. "I do love playing historical figures simply because there's so much incredibly diverse, interesting information about a character when you can research their life," he explained to Back Stage. "A lot of the stuff you'd never be able to make up as a writer."

In 2012, DiCaprio appeared as a slave owner in Quentin Tarantino's western Django Unchained, co-starring Jamie Foxx, Kerry Washington and Christoph Waltz. The following year, he re-teamed with Luhrmann to play one of literature's most intriguing characters, starring as Jay Gatsby in the adaptation of the F. Scott Fitzgerald classic The Great Gatsby.

DiCaprio again joined forces with Scorsese in the 2013 drama The Wolf of Wall Street, based on the memoir by Jordan Belfort, who gained notoriety for defrauding investors while lining his own pockets in the 1990s. DiCaprio's portrayal of Belfort earned him a Golden Globe for best actor, along with Academy Award nominations as both actor and producer. Jonah Hill and Matthew McConaughey also starred in the film.

In 2015 it was announced that DiCaprio and Scorsese would be partnering up again to work on the film adaptation of Erik Larson's The Devil in the White City, in which the actor would play the 19th-century serial killer H.H. Holmes. That year DiCaprio also starred in the thriller The Revenant, earning a slew of acclaim for his portrayal of Hugh Glass, an 1820s frontiersman forced to endure the wilderness after being left for dead.

Directed by Alejandro González Iñárritu, the film was difficult to shoot due to frigid weather but has garnered major interest among the public and critics. The

Revenant was widely released in the U.S. during the second weekend of January, earning more than $39 million. That same weekend DiCaprio, Iñárritu and the film itself received Golden Globes in the categories of best actor, director and drama, respectively. Upon winning, the popular DiCaprio received a standing ovation from his peers and praised Iñárritu for his vision while also calling for support to indigenous communities and the protection of natural environments. A few days later, DiCaprio received another lead actor Academy Award nod, with The Revenant picking up 12 nominations in total. In February 2016, DiCaprio won the first Oscar of his career, making a plaintive call to honor the environment and indigenous rights.

"Making The Revenant was about man's relationship to the natural world. A world that we collectively felt in 2015 as the hottest year in recorded history. Our production needed to move to the southern tip of this planet just to be able to find snow. Climate change is real, it is happening right now," DiCaprio said towards the end of his Academy Award acceptance speech. "It is the most urgent threat facing our entire species, and we need to work collectively together and stop procrastinating. We need to support leaders around the world who do not speak for the big polluters, but who speak for all of humanity, for the indigenous people of the world, for the billions and billions of underprivileged people out there who would be most affected by this."

As reflected by his Globe and Oscar speeches, DiCaprio has long demonstrated his passion for environmental issues. In 2000, he hosted an Earth Day celebration and interviewed former U.S. President Bill Clinton for a television segment about global warming. DiCaprio also wrote, narrated and produced The 11th Hour, an environmental documentary that was released in 2007.

The actor is one of the founders of The Leonardo DiCaprio Fund at California Community Foundation, a nonprofit that supports and brings awareness to numerous environmental causes. He's also served on the boards of the World Wildlife Fund, the Natural Resources Defense Council and the International Fund for Animal Welfare.

During much of his career, DiCaprio has found himself in the media spotlight for his personal life. His on-again, off-again relationship with supermodel Gisele Bündchen was fodder for celebrity magazines and websites from 2000 to 2005. DiCaprio then dated model Bar Refaeli for several years. In 2011, he was briefly linked to actress Blake Lively. Since then, he's reportedly dated various models.

Roman Abramovich

Roman Arkadyevich Abramovich is a Russian business tycoon, one of the richest men in the world and owner of the Chelsea Football Club.

The 45 year-old is the ninth-richest man in Russia and the 53rd-richest man in the world with an estimated net worth of $13.4 billion, according to the Forbes rich list 2011

Roman Arkadyevich Abramovich was born on October 24, 1966 in Saratov, S Russia. Orphaned at age two, he was raised by an uncle. While a student, Abramovich set up a toy production company which he eventually parlayed into a fortune in the oil industry. Now, one of the richest men in the world, Abramovich is owner of the Chelsea Football Club and of private investment firm, Millhouse LLC.

Far from the glamour of Knightsbridge, West London, where he owns a £150 million eight-bedroom palace, Abramovich spent his childhood in the desolate region of Komi in the Russian Arctic circle. The harsh region has long periods of darkness in the winter and thick permafrost hiding vast reserves of oil.

Abramovich, who was born in Lithuania, was orphaned at a young age. His Jewish parents Irina and Arkady died before he was four and he was raised by his grandparents.

Abramovich dropped out of two colleges and served in the army before appearing in Moscow as a right-hand man to Boris Berezovsky. Berezovsky wielded huge power under President Boris Yeltsin and amassed billions in the ruthless carve-up of the crumbling Soviet Union's industrial assets.

Multi-billionaire businessman and entrepreneur Roman Abramovich was born in Saratov, S Russia. Born into impoverished circumstances and orphaned at age two, he was raised by an uncle and his family in Ukhta, N Russia. While still a student at the Moscow Auto Transport Institute (1987), he set up a small company producing plastic toys, and its success enabled him to found an oil business in the Omsk region. He rapidly made a name for himself within the industry and joined the board of the Sibneft company, eventually taking sole charge, and completing a merger which made it the fourth biggest oil company in the world. Sibneft was sold to the state-run Russian gas company, Gazprom, in 2005. In 1999 he was elected to the lower house of the Russian parliament representing the isolated Siberian area of Chukotka, to which he has donated large sums for improvement schemes. He was re-elected for a second term in 2005. Among his many homes is a country estate in Sussex, and he has become a familiar face in England since his acquisition of Chelsea Football Club in 2003.

Dhirubhai Ambani

Dhirajlal Hirachand Ambani(Dhirubhai Ambani) was born on 28 December 1932, at Chorwad, Junagadh (now the state of Gujarat, India) to Hirachand Gordhanbhai Ambani and Jamnaben in a Modh family of very moderate means.He was the second son of a school teacher.

Dhirubhai Ambani is said to have started his entrepreneurial career by selling "pakora" to pilgrims in Mount Girnar over the weekends. When he was 16 years old, he moved to Aden, Yemen. He worked with A. Besse & Co. for a salary of Rs.300. Two years later, A. Besse & Co. became the distributors for Shell products, and Dhirubhai was promoted to manage the company's filling station at the port of Aden.

He was married to Kokilaben and had two sons, Mukesh Ambani and Anil Ambani and two daughters, Nina Kothari and Deepti Salgaocar.

In 1962, Dhirubhai returned to India and started the Reliance Commercial Corporation with a capital of Rs.15, 000.00. The primary business of Reliance Commercial Corporation was to import polyester yarn and export spices.The first office of the Reliance Commercial Corporation was set up at the Narsinathan Street in Masjid Bunder. It was a 350 Sq. Ft. room with a telephone, one table and three chairs. Initially, they had two assistants to help them with their business. In 1965, Champaklal Damani and Dhirubhai Ambani ended their partnership and Dhirubhai started on his own. It is believed that both had different temperaments and a different take on how to conduct business. While Mr. Damani was a cautious trader and did not believe in building yarn inventories, Dhirubhai was a known risk taker and he considered that building inventories, anticipating a price rise, and making profits through that was good for growth.

During this period, Dhirubhai and his family used to stay in one bedroom apartment at the Jaihind Estate in Bhuleshwar, Mumbai. In 1968, he moved to an upmarket apartment at Altamount Road in South Mumbai. Ambani's net worth was estimated at about Rs.1 million by late 1960s.

Ambani's his great achievement was that he showed Indians what was possible. With no Oxford or Yale degree and no family capital, he achieved what the Elite "brown sahibs" of New Delhi could not: he built an ultramodern, profitable, global enterprise in India itself. What's more, he enlisted four million Indians, a generation weaned on nanny-state socialism, in an adventure in can-do capitalism, convincing them to load up on Reliance stock.

Still, Ambani seems destined to be remembered as a folk hero—an example of what a man from one of India's poor villages can accomplish with non-shrink ambition.

Steve Jobs

Steve Jobs was born on February 24, 1955, in the city of San Francisco. His biological mother was either an unwed graduate student named Joanne Simpson, and his biological father was a political science or mathematics professor, a native Syrian named Abdulfattah John Jandali.

Being born out of wedlock in the puritan America of the 1950s, the baby was put up for adoption. Joanne had a college education, and she insisted that the future parents of her boy be just as well educated. Unfortunately, the candidates, Paul and Clara Jobs, did not meet her expectations: they were a lower-middle class couple that had settled in the Bay Area after the war. Paul was a machinist from the Midwest who had not even graduated from high school. In the end, Joanne agreed to have her baby adopted by them, under the firm condition that they later send him to college.

Paul and Clara called their son Steven Paul. While Steve was still a toddler, the couple moved to the Santa Clara county, later to be known as Silicon Valley. They adopted another baby, a girl called Patti, three years later in 1958.

Steve was quite a turbulent child. He really didn't care about school for some time — until he reached the 4th grade, and had Imogene "Teddy" Hill as a teacher.

She was one of the saints of my life. She taught an advanced fourth grade class, and it took her about a month to get hip to my situation. She bribed me into learning.

She did bribe him, with candy and $5 bills from her own money. He quickly became hooked — so much so that he skipped the 5th grade and went straight to middle school, namely Crittenden Middle School. It was in a poor area. Most kids did not work much there, they were rather fond of bullying other kids, such as the young Steve. One day he came home and declared that if he wasn't transferred to another school, he would stop going to school altogether. He was 11. Paul and Clara complied, and the Jobses moved to the cozier city of Los Altos, so that Steve could go to Cupertino Junior High. This proved to be decisive for Steve's future.

The Santa Clara county, south of San Francisco, California, was a bourgeoning place for computer engineering as early as the 1960s. Indeed, after the Soviet Union launched Sputnik in 1957, the country engaged in the Space Race, and billions of dollars of federal money were poured into technology companies to advance the state of the art of computing.

One of those firms was the Shockley Semiconductor Company, from William Schockley, who got the Nobel Prize of Physics in 1956 for inventing the transistor. Another dominant firm was Hewlett Packard, founded in Palo Alto in 1939. HP was a company of engineers, selling products to engineers. There were tons of them scattered all over this valley of apricot orchards.

As Steve was growing up in Los Altos, he became increasingly curious about the world of electronics that filled his neighbors' garages. His own father introduced him to Heathkits, which fascinated him:

These Heathkits would come with these detailed manuals about how to put this thing together and all the parts would be laid out in a certain way and color coded. You'd actually build this thing yourself. I would say that this gave one several things. It gave one a understanding of what was inside a finished product and how it worked because it would include a theory of operation but maybe even more importantly it gave one the sense that one could build the things that one saw around oneself in the universe. These things were not mysteries anymore. I mean you looked at a television set you would think that "I haven't built one of those but I could. There's one of those in the Heathkit catalog and I've built two other Heathkits so I could build that." Things became much more clear that they were the results of human creation not these magical things that just appeared in one's environment that one had no knowledge of their interiors.

It gave a tremendous level of self-confidence, that through exploration and learning one could understand seemingly very complex things in one's environment. My childhood was very fortunate in that way.

When Steve arrived in Homestead High School, he enrolled in a popular electronics class. McCollum later recalled of one time when his pupil Steve called up Bill Hewlett himself, co-founder of HP, to get spare parts for his homework, and even a summer job at HP's factory. Steve's entrepreneurial skills showed up early in his life indeed.

At Homestead, Steve befriended Bill Fernandez, a neighbor who shared his interests in electronics. It was Bill who first introduced him to another computer whiz kid, an older guy named Stephen Wozniak, or — as everybody used to call him — Woz. Steve and Woz met in 1969, when they were respectively 14 and 19. At the time, Woz was building a little computer board with Bill Fernandez that they called "the Cream Soda Computer". Woz showed it to Steve, who seemed quite interested.

Typically, it was really hard for me to explain to people the kind of design stuff I worked on, but Steve got it right away. And I liked him. He was kind of skinny and wiry and full of energy. [...] Steve and I got close right away, even though he was still in high school [...]. We talked electronics, we talked about music we liked, and we traded stories about pranks we'd pulled.

Woz and Steve later engaged in several pranks together, including putting a huge middle finger on one of the high school's building.

It was also at Homestead that Steve met Chris-Ann Brennan, his first steady girlfriend, with whom he stayed for several years.

A couple of years later, Woz and Steve started their first entrepreneurial venture. It was 1972, and on US campuses, there was a lot of talk about "phone phreaks." They were early computer hackers that managed to build "blue boxes" — little devices that fooled AT&T's long-distance switching equipment, and allowed you to make phone calls for free.

Woz read about them in an article which he showed to Steve. They both tried to build one, and to their surprise, it worked! It was Steve who came up with the idea of selling them; he and Woz would go from room to room in Berkeley's dorms, where Woz was a student, and sell them to interested students. However, this business was illegal and the two of them stopped after they almost got caught by the police.

The following year, Steve finished high school and reached college age. He decided to go to the fancy Reed College, a private liberal arts college up in Oregon. However, the tuition for Reed was so expensive that Paul and Clara could hardly afford it. Yet they were bound by the promise they'd make to their son's biological mother, so they spent almost their entire life's savings on their son's higher education.

Steve only officially stayed for a couple of months at Reed. He dropped out before Christmas. However, that allowed him to "drop in" on classes he was not supposed to attend.

After six months, I couldn't see the value in it. I had no idea what I wanted to do with my life and no idea how college was going to help me figure it out. And here I was spending all of the money my parents had saved their entire life. So I decided to drop out and trust that it would all work out OK. It was pretty scary at the time, but looking back it was one of the best decisions I ever made. The minute I dropped out I could stop taking the required classes that didn't interest me, and begin dropping in on the ones that looked interesting.

It wasn't all romantic. I didn't have a dorm room, so I slept on the floor in friends' rooms, I returned coke bottles for the 5¢ deposits to buy food with, and I would walk the 7 miles across town every Sunday night to get one good meal a week at the Hare Krishna temple. I loved it.

It was at Reed that Steve started experimenting with Eastern mysticism. He delved into weird books and came to believe that if he ate only fruits, for example, he would eliminate all mucus and not need to shower anymore. He also started his habit of fasting for long periods of time (he would still do so ten years later, when he was a multi-millionaire). He occasionally used LSD, and became something of a laggard hippie. One of his best friends at Reed was Dan Kottke, who shared his interests in such philosophies.

The following year, in 1974, Steve desperately needed money, so he got a job at Atari. Atari was arguably the first video game company: it was created by Nolan Bushnell in 1972, and one of its first employees was Al Acorn, the inventor of Pong. Steve was hired although he would often call his co-workers names and smell pretty bad. That's why he was soon moved to the night shift.

Young Steve Jobs looked up to Atari's founder Nolan Bushnell. He was impressed by this iconoclastic man who made a lot of money by building pinball machines. He was clearly an inspiration for him to start Apple.

While he was at Atari, Steve asked his boss to fund a trip to India for him. Atari did pay his trip up to Germany, where he had to work on fixing some Atari machines. Then Steve was joined by his hippie friend from Reed, Dan Kottke, and they went to India in search for enlightenment. They came back pretty disappointed, especially after they met a famous guru, Kairolie Baba, who, unlike what they expected, was a con man.

We weren't going to find a place where we could go for a month to be enlightened. It was one of the first times that I started to realize that maybe Thomas Edison did a lot more to improve the world than Karl Marx and Neem Kairolie Baba put together.

When Steve came back, he resumed his job at Atari. One of his pastimes back then included primal scream therapy sessions at the Los Altos Zen Center, where he befriended Governor Jerry Brown and his guru Kobun Chino. He also spent several weeks with his girlfriend Chris-Ann and Dan Kottke in a hippie commune in Oregon, the All-One Farm. Here they would cultivate apples and for some time, Steve would eat only that — when he wasn't fasting, that is.

While Steve had been away in India or Oregon, his geek friend Woz had been hired by Hewlett-Packard. To him, it was a dream job: a company full of passionate engineers just like him, where he could work on products for other engineers. However, in his spare time, he had cultivated his interest in designing computer circuits, and had joined a computer hobbyists association called the Homebrew Computer Club.

Computers existed for a long time before Apple was started. For example, arguably one of the first full-blown US computers ever built was ENIAC, in 1946. By the 1970s, the majority of large corporations were already equipped with computers. But those were usually huge mainframes in giant computer rooms, built and maintained by industry behemoth IBM.

Personal computing was based on a radically different approach. It claimed that computers could be used by mere mortals, private individuals instead of institutions. It was a revolutionary idea, and it's no surprise it emerged in the Bay Area in the 1970s, after the hippie revolution and at the heartland of the electronics industry.

It all started in 1974, when Mountain View-based Intel introduced the world's first microprocessor, the 8080. All sorts of hobbyists started to get interested in how to use this powerful yet relatively cheap new piece of technology. A huge leap forward was made when a man named Ed Roberts launched the Altair, out of Albuberque, New Mexico. It was a computer kit based on the 8080, which people could assemble by themselves, a lot like the Heathkits Steve Jobs worked on in his childhood.

The Altair was basically a box that could flash lights on and off. It didn't do much until Bill Gates and Paul Allen, who had just founded a new company called Microsoft, wrote a BASIC interpreter for it in 1975. The word spread around all over the country in those personal computing circles (which mostly consisted of engineers, radio amateurs and other types of nerds). The Homebrew Computer Club, which operated from Stanford's Linear Accelerator Center auditorium, was one of those groups. Hobbysits would go there to show off their latest machine or program they had worked on.

Woz was impressed by the Altair (and by Microsoft's BASIC interpreter), but he knew from his almost life-long experience in circuit design that he could do a much better job. So he started work on his own computer — which he decided to base on another microprocessor, MOS's Technology 502. This was his new goal in life. While keeping his job at HP, he worked very hard at this computer board, and came up with an impressive result; a powerful computer (for the time) which worked with a keyboard and screen, not one that flashed lights — and all with amazingly few chips.

Woz showed his computer design to his friend Steve Jobs. Steve was impressed. He did not know much about engineering, but he could see there was a demand for having a computer to write software for, a computer for software hobbyists. He was especially excited to see that a lot of the qualified engineers at Homebrew were talking about Woz's computer with admiration. So he suggested to sell it to them. He and Woz would assemble the computers themselves and sell the whole board at Homebrew meetings.

Steve had a good argument. We were in his car and he said — and I can remember him saying this like it was yesterday: "Well, even if we lose money, we'll have a company. For once in our lives, we'll have a company." That convinced me. And I was excited to think about us like that. To be two best friends starting a company.

To get the necessary $1,000 to start building the first boards, Steve sold his Volkswagen van, and Woz his HP 65 calculator. They thought about how to call the new company, and couldn't come up with a good name, until one day, Steve said that they would call it Apple if they didn't find anything better. And they didn't — so Apple Computer was born.

The two friends sought help, and they got it from one of Steve's colleagues from Atari, Ron Wayne. Wayne basically wrote the necessary paperwork to start a corporation and drew the company's first logo. As a result, he got 10% of the company's shares, while Steve and Woz split the rest (45% each).

Another problem was that Woz was still working for HP, and under the terms of his contract, all his work belonged to the corporation. The Apple computer was technically HP property. But Woz showed it to his bosses and they simply didn't care about it. Woz was disappointed as his goal was to work for HP his whole life. He would have been delighted if HP had done a personal computer based on his design. It wasn't Steve Jobs' intention though.

Apple Computer's first order was from a Homebrew member called Paul Terrel. He was starting a new computer store called the Byte Shop, in Mountain View, and understood just like Steve that there was a demand for such fully-built computers. He ordered 50 of them, at $500 a piece. That was $25,000! It was a huge starting point for the young company, and got Steve and Woz very excited. They started putting together the parts in the Jobses's garage, with help from Steve's sister Patti and his friend from Reed, Dan Kottke. They paid them $1 a board. The parts for the Apple cost $220, while the computer was sold to Terrel for $500, who would usually put it in wooden boxes.

Steve and Woz also started selling the computer on their own. They agreed on the retail price of $666.66 (note that his price was based on a simple calculation — a 33% margin — and had nothing to do with the Satanic number of course). They showed it to the Homebrew folks in March 1976, but the response wasn't that enthusiastic. So they went elsewhere, going from store to store and trying to sell them. They sold a couple hundreds this way.

This was the start of Apple Computer. Steve and Woz had bought the other co-founder Ron Wayne out for $800, and incorporated the company on April 1, 1976.

The day he finished work on his first computer, Woz started working on an improved design, the future Apple II. The Apple II was based on the Apple I's design, but in many ways it was a huge breakthrough.

First, it ran a lot faster with half as many chips. It also was the first computer that could produce color, with any color TV you would plug it into. It could handle high-resolution graphics and sound, and had a BASIC interpreter built-in. In short, it was the first computer that anybody who knew the BASIC programming language could use: it had what it took to launch the personal computing revolution.

The prototype for the Apple II was almost ready when Steve and Woz partook in the Personal Computer Festival, held in Atlantic City in the summer of 1976. But it was not ready enough to be shown to the public. Steve and his friend Dan Kottke were trying to sell the Apple I from their Apple Computer booth, while Woz was working on finishing the Apple II. The visitors were not impressed by the Apple I, a board sold by these two amateur bearded young men, while MITS, which sold the Altair, had a huge booth with music, dancers and business suits. Steve learned a lot that day.

After the Apple II was finished, Steve went looking for investors. He talked to several venture capitalists, who were already legions in the Valley. The first to show up was Don Valentine. He turned Steve and Woz down, but he did give them a hand by passing them the name of another potential investor, Mike Markkula. Mike was a former Intel employee who had made millions and retired early. He was 34 when he met with Woz and Steve, and he bought into their vision. He was also quite aware of the potential returns on his investment:

We're going to be a Fortune 500 company in two years. This is the start of an industry. It happens once a decade.

Mike drew up a business plan. He wanted to put in $250,000 to build 1,000 machines. This was a huge number by the young men's standards. Woz was also told that for this to happen, he had to leave HP. At first he refused, since he was a huge admirer of HP and planned to work there his whole life. But Steve lobbied him hard into it, and in the end Woz relented.

Mike Markkula also insisted that Apple advertise for its new computer. He called up one of his friends, Regis McKenna, who was one of the most renowned advertisers in the Valley. While they worked with Steve Jobs on Apple's first ads, an art director called Rob Janoff designed a new logo for the company. The only thing Steve asked him was: "Don't make it cute." He was the one who came up with the bitten apple (so that it wouldn't look like a tomato), as well as the striped colors — to emphasize the Apple II's ability to display color.

Rod Holt, a friend of Steve Jobs', was hired to build a switching power supply and design a mold for the Apple II's plastic case. Mike Markkula later also hired a fourth guy, Mike Scott, to run the startup, whose first offices were moved to Stevens Creek Boulevard in Cupertino.

The new company got ready to show off their product at the West Coast Computer Faire, a conference held in San Francisco in April 1977. It was only a prototype, but the plastic case definitely made the Apple II look like a professional product. Steve negotiated a prime spot for Apple's booth, and took precious advice from both Mike Markkula and Regis McKenna. That's why he bought his first suit for the occasion.

Apple Computer received 300 orders for the Apple II on the show alone, twice as much as the total number of Apple I's ever sold! But this was just the beginning.

J.K. Rowling

J.K. Rowling is the creator of the Harry Potter fantasy series, one of the most popular book and film franchises in history.

"I was set free because my greatest fear had been realized and I still had a daughter that I adored, and I had an old typewriter and a big idea. And so rock bottom became a solid foundation on which I rebuilt my life."

—J.K. Rowling

J.K. Rowling - Mini Biography (TV-14; 4:18) A short biography of J.K. Rowling whose "Harry Potter" books have become the bestselling book series in history.

Born in Yate, England, on July 31, 1965, J.K. Rowling came from humble economic means before writing Harry Potter and the Sorcerer's Stone, a children's fantasy novel. The work was an international hit and Rowling wrote six more books in the series, which sold hundreds of millions of copies and was adapted into a blockbuster film franchise. In 2012, Rowling released the novel The Casual Vacancy.

Joanne Rowling, best known as J.K. Rowling, was born on July 31, 1965, in Yate, England. She adopted her pen name, J.K., incorporating her grandmother's name, Kathleen, for the latter initial (Rowling does not have a middle name).

As a single mother living in Edinburgh, Scotland, Rowling became an international literary sensation in 1999, when the first three installments of her Harry Potter children's book series took over the top three slots of The New York Times best-seller list after achieving similar success in her native United Kingdom. The phenomenal response to Rowling's books culminated in July 2000, when the fourth volume in the series, Harry Potter and the Goblet of Fire, became the fastest-selling book in history.

A graduate of Exeter University, Rowling moved to Portugal in 1990 to teach English. There, she met and married the Portuguese journalist Jorge Arantes. The couple's daughter, Jessica, was born in 1993. After her marriage ended in divorce, Rowling moved to Edinburgh with her daughter to live near her younger sister, Di. While struggling to support Jessica and herself on welfare, Rowling worked on a book, the idea for which had reportedly occurred to her while she was traveling on a train from Manchester to London in 1990. After a number of rejections, she finally sold the book, Harry Potter and the Philosopher's Stone (the word "Philosopher" was changed to "Sorcerer" for its publication in America), for the equivalent of about $4,000. The book, and its subseqent series, chronicled the life of Harry Potter, a young wizard, and his motley band of cohorts at the Hogwarts School of Witchcraft and Wizardry.

By the summer of 2000, the first three Harry Potter books, Harry Potter and the Sorcerer's Stone, Harry Potter and the Chamber of Secrets and Harry Potter and the Prisoner of Azkaban earned approximately $480 million in three years, with over 35 million copies in print in 35 languages. In July 2000, Harry Potter and the Goblet of Fire saw a first printing of 5.3 million copies and advance orders of over 1.8 million. After a postponed release date, the fifth installment, Harry Potter and the Order of the Phoenix, hit bookstores in June 2003. The sixth installment, Harry Potter and the Half-Blood Prince, sold 6.9 million copies in the United States in its first 24 hours, the biggest opening in publishing history. Prior to its July 2007 release, the seventh and final installment in the Harry Potter series, Harry Potter and the Deathly Hallows, was the largest ever pre-ordered book at Barnes & Noble and Borders bookstores, and at Amazon.com.

Rowling, now Britain's 13th wealthiest woman—wealthier than even the Queen—does not plan to write any more books in the series, but has not entirely ruled out the possibility.

A film version of Harry Potter and the Sorcerer's Stone, directed by Chris Columbus and starring Daniel Radcliffe, Emma Watson and Rupert Grint, was released in November 2001. In its opening weekend in the U.S., the film debuted on a record 8,200 screens and smashed the previous box-office record, earning an estimated $93.5 million ($20 million more than the previous recordholder, 1999's The Lost World: Jurassic Park). It ended the year as the top-grossing movie of 2001. The second and third films in the series — Harry Potter and the Chamber of Secrets (2002) directed by Columbus and Harry Potter and the Prisoner of Azkaban (2004) directed by Alfonso Cuarón — each enjoyed similar record-breaking box-office success. Harry Potter and the Goblet of Fire, directed by Mike Newell, was released in 2005. The fifth movie, Harry Potter and the Order of the Phoenix, directed by David Yates, was released in 2007, featuring a script by screenwriter Michael Goldenberg, who replaced Steve Kloves, writer of the first four films. The film version of Harry Potter and the Half-Blood Prince, directed by Yates, was released in July 2009, followed by the final film which was released in two installments — Harry Potter and the Deathly Hallows Part 1 (2010) and Part 2 (2011), also directed by Yates.

Although J.K. Rowling's Harry Potter series is finished, the author continues to work on more written works. The Tales of Beedle the Bard, a collection of five fables mentioned in the Harry Potter book series, was released on November 4, 2008—at a tea party for 200 schoolchildren at the National Library of Scotland in Edinburgh. Rowling donated all royalties from the book to the Children's High

Level Group (which has been renamed Lumos), a charity that Rowling co-founded to support institutionalized children in Eastern Europe.

Rowling's first book aimed at adults, The Casual Vacancy, was published in September 2012. The novel, a dark comedy about a local election in the small English town of Pagford, received mixed reviews. A book review in The New York Times called the novel "disappointing" and "dull." A review in The Telegraph, however, gave the book three out of five stars, stating that the novel is " . . .Jane Austen herself would admire the way [Rowling] shows the news of Barry's death spreading like a virus round Pagford."

In 2013, Rowling broke into a new genre: crime fiction. But this new work involved a mystery all of its own. She published the mystery novel Cuckoo Calling that April under the pen name Robert Galbraith. In its first few months of release, the novel had modest sales and received positive reviews. Sales for the work skyrocketed in July when its author's identity was discovered. According to Bloomberg News, Rowling said that "I had hoped to keep this secret a little longer, because being Robert Galbraith has been such a liberating experience. It has been wonderful to publish without hype or expectation, and pure pleasure to get feedback under a different name."

Later that year, Rowling announced a new film series with Warner Bros. The first film in the series, which was released in November 2016, features a script by Rowling, her screenwriting debut, which is based on her Hogwarts textbook Fantastic Beasts and Where to Find Them. According to Entertainment Weekly, Rowling explained that the movies, which star Eddie Redmayne, draw from "the worldwide community of witches and wizards where I was so happy for 17 years," but "is neither a prequel nor a sequel to the Harry Potter series, but an extension of the wizarding world."

Rowling is also reportedly working on a new Harry Potter-related book. On her website, she announced that she will write "an encyclopedia of Harry's world" and the royalties from this volume will be donated to charity.

In 2014, Rowling published a short story about grown-up Harry Potter and a Hogwarts school reunion on her website Pottermore. Since the site launched, she's added more stories and information about all things Harry Potter.

In June 2016, Harry Potter and the Cursed Child, a two-part play written by by Jack Thorne and director John Tiffany and based on Rowling's story, debuted on the London stage to a sold-out audience. Although she had originally stated Harry Potter and the Deathly Hallows would be the final book in the series, the play features an adult Harry Potter and has been officially touted as the eight installment of the series. The play's cast differs from that of the original films. The next month, as with her previous books, fans lined up at book stores pending the midnight release of Jack Thorne's script for Harry Potter and the Cursed Child.

On December 26, 2001, J.K. Rowling married anesthetist Dr. Neil Murray at the couple's home in Scotland. They have two children together, David (born in 2003) and Mackenzie (born in 2005). Rowling has one child, Jessica (born 1993), from her previous marriage.

Charlie Chaplin

Charles Spencer Chaplin was born in London, England, on April 16th, 1889. His father was a versatile vocalist and actor; and his mother, known under the stage name of Lily Harley, was an attractive actress and singer, who gained a reputation for her work in the light opera field.

Charlie was thrown on his own resources before he reached the age of ten as the early death of his father and the subsequent illness of his mother made it necessary for Charlie and his brother, Sydney, to fend for themselves.

Having inherited natural talents from their parents, the youngsters took to the stage as the best opportunity for a career. Charlie made his professional debut as a member of a juvenile group called "The Eight Lancashire Lads" and rapidly won popular favour as an outstanding tap dancer.

When he was about twelve, he got his first chance to act in a legitimate stage show, and appeared as "Billy" the page boy, in support of William Gillette in "Sherlock Holmes". At the close of this engagement, Charlie started a career as a comedian in vaudeville, which eventually took him to the United States in 1910 as a featured player with the Fred Karno Repertoire Company.

He scored an immediate hit with American audiences, particularly with his characterization in a sketch entitled "A Night in an English Music Hall". When the Fred Karno troupe returned to the United States in the fall of 1912 for a repeat tour, Chaplin was offered a motion picture contract.

He finally agreed to appear before the cameras at the expiration of his vaudeville commitments in November 1913; and his entrance in the cinema world took place that month when he joined Mack Sennett and the Keystone Film Company. His initial salary was $150 a week, but his overnight success on the screen spurred other producers to start negotiations for his services.

At the completion of his Sennett contract, Chaplin moved on to the Essanay Company (1915) at a large increase. Sydney Chaplin had then arrived from England, and took his brother's place with Keystone as their leading comedian.

The following year Charlie was even more in demand and signed with the Mutual Film Corporation for a much larger sum to make 12 two-reel comedies. These include "The Floorwalker", "The Fireman", "The Vagabond", "One A.M." (a production in which he was the only character for the entire two reels with the exception of the entrance of a cab driver in the opening scene), "The Count", "The Pawnshop", "Behind the Screen", "The Rink", "Easy Street" (heralded as his greatest production up to that time), "The Cure", "The Immigrant" and "The Adventurer".

When his contract with Mutual expired in 1917, Chaplin decided to become an independent producer in a desire for more freedom and greater leisure in making his movies. To that end, he busied himself with the construction of his own studios. This plant was situated in the heart of the residential section of Hollywood at La Brea Avenue.

Early in 1918, Chaplin entered into an agreement with First National Exhibitors' Circuit, a new organization specially formed to exploit his pictures. His first film under this new deal was "A Dog's Life". After this production, he turned his attention to a national tour on behalf of the war effort, following which he made a film the US government used to popularize the Liberty Loan drive: "The Bond".

His next commercial venture was the production of a comedy dealing with the war. "Shoulder Arms", released in 1918 at a most opportune time, proved a veritable mirthquake at the box office and added enormously to Chaplin's popularity.

He followed "Shoulder Arms" with "Sunnyside" and "A Day's Pleasure", both released in 1919. In April of that year, Chaplin joined with Mary Pickford, Douglas Fairbanks and D.W. Griffith to found the United Artists Corporation. B.B. Hampton, in his "History of the Movies" says:

"The corporation was organized as a distributor, each of the artists retaining entire control of his or her respective producing activities, delivering to United Artists the completed pictures for distribution on the same general plan they would have followed with a distributing organization which they did not own. The stock of United Artists was divided equally among the founders. This arrangement introduced a new method into the industry. Heretofore, producers and distributors had been the employers, paying salaries and sometimes a share of the profits to the stars. Under the United Artists system, the stars became their own employers. They had to do their own financing, but they received the producer profits that had formerly gone to their employers and each received his share of the profits of the distributing organization."

So, read all that? Or, probably, skipped most of the above! I knew. But, that's ok! Yes, our mission was NOT to read the biographies, but to get to know the *IDEAS* they used to be at such a position that there biographies are being widely written and read across the world!

Well, there is one thing in common in all above bios, and you would have noticed that if you really read them!

Hard-work and good fortune are the two most important things you need to get there.

Don't have any luck? No problem!

You would have heard the saying,

"The only thing that overcomes hard-luck is hard-work!"

Not heard, yet? I have told you now, haven't I?

So keep this book in your bookshelf for now, or lend it to a friend who wants to be rich, and begin planning for your own success-story!

I think you liked the collection, don't you?

Oh, I forgot that step-by-step guide which I promised in the beginning. Here it goes:

The Step-by-Step Guide to
Becoming Rich!

By Sanyam Sadana

Saving:

Saving money is one of the most important skills on the path to wealth. While the saying "a penny saved is a penny earned" is true to an extent, in reality, a penny saved may equal a dollar earned over time if you properly invest your saved money.

Saving money requires one thing — to spend less than you take in. This is easier to do if you have a solid income (which is why investing in education is important), but it is important to remember that it is possible to save money regardless of your income, even if the amounts are small.

Try to start by saving 15% of your paycheck each month. While the recommended goal is 25%, begin with 10% or 15%, if this is not possible, simply save what you can, with the goal being to add something to your savings each month.

A solid budget is the first step on the path to wealth. It helps you to identify all your expenses, and therefore control and reduce them. This, in turn, allows you to save your money which gives you capital to invest with.

On a sheet of paper or in a word processing document, list all your income for the course of a month in one column. At the bottom, add up the sources to determine a total.

In another column, do the same for expenses. Make sure to include everything. One helpful way to do this is to examine your bank statement and credit card statement. Add all the expenses in the column together to determine the total monthly expenses.

Look closely at the expense column to find areas to reduce spending. Your goal should be to create more "space" between the total number in the income column, and the total number in the expense column.

One way to do this is to examine the difference between "wants", and "needs". A want is essential, whereas as a need is option. Look to your "wants" each month to find reductions. For example, you may want a brand new kindle fire or voyage with books worth twenty dollars or so, while you only need a basic kindle with low priced e-books.

Before you invest at all, always have an emergency savings fund prepared. Experts recommend having at least three months of living expenses set aside in case of a job loss, medical emergency, or unexpected expense.

After an emergency fund is prepared, you can then focus on using your savings to build your investment portfolio.

bout half of American workplaces have access to something called a 401(k), which is a special plan whereby some money is deducted every month from your check and invested. Often, your employer will match all or a portion of your contribution.

The benefit of a 401(k) is that your money can grow tax-free (normally taxes are charged and collected annually on invested money which makes it grow slower). In addition, money you contribute is tax-deductible. This means if you contribute $5,000, you won't pay income tax on that money.

Inquire at your workplace if a 401(k) plan is available, and make sure to take advantage of it, especially if your employer offers matching contributions. This is an excellent way to get started on a path to wealth.

Now start earning seriously, if you don't. Ask yourself what your talents are. Consider the things you do better than other people, or that you are frequently complimented on.

Ask yourself what you are passionate about, or interested in. For example, maybe a particular subject interests you, like mathematics, or a particular activity, like cooking.

Look for areas of overlap between your talents, and your interests. For example, maybe you are interested in the human body, and also are good at math or science. These interests can complement each other.

For better or worse, some fields simply pay more than others, and are in higher demand. The best situation is to have one of these higher-paying fields or occupations match your skills and interests. If not, consider exploring these fields anyways to see if you can develop an interest.

Currently some of the best paying university undergraduate majors are engineering, computer science and business/economics. These majors all lead to average salaries above $75,000 per year.

If you already have a university degree and want to pursue further education, careers like law, medicine or dentistry can produce salaries well over $100,000 per year.

Make sure to consider skilled trades as well for a career. If you are a more "hands-on" person, there is considerable money that can be made in learning a skilled trade. Plumbers and HVAC technicians can earn over $50,000 per year, and the earning potential is unlimited if you start your own business.

Before you choose an educational path, research what the job prospects are currently and when you will enter the field, and what the average salary is. Remember, a popular field today may be saturated in 5 to 10 years. This will help you make sure you can get a return on your investment.

Unfortunately, educating yourself costs money, but if you choose a wise major, you are very likely to earn your investment back, plus much more.

Consider spending a year or two before you start school to save some money. This will reduce the amount you need to borrow, which means you will have smaller loan repayments when you are done.

Choose your base of operations wisely. Unless you very much enjoy living in a big city or have family/other obligations, choose a less expensive area in which to live and go to school. Choosing a smaller city can lead to thousands in saved living expenses.

Apply for federal student loans to fund your education. These loans often have lower interest rates than bank loans, the interest rates are often fixed, and you do not need to repay until you are done with school.

Increase your professional skills, leadership skills, financial skills, social skills and general life skills. Making––and keeping–– yourself valuable will increase your chances on whatever path you take. Continuous self-development will enable you to make better use of your financial assets.

Adding to your education constantly means adding to your earning potential. Every new thing you learn increases your ability to earn.

That's it. Simple, yeah! So, what are you waiting for? Start your journey to success now! (And, as I told you, advice your friends to buy this book if they wish to be rich! I too want to become rich, yeah!)

www.ingramcontent.com/pod-product-compliance
Lightning Source LLC
Chambersburg PA
CBHW051722170526
45167CB00002B/762